# RECYCLED HEARTS

 STARRING "LOTTERY WINNER" CATS
BY DEE E. FELL
PHOTOS BY DEE E. FELL
ILLUSTRATIONS BY
FRITZ FELL AND
DEE E. FELL

Illustrations: Page 24 and cat on Cover by Fritz Fell

Copyright 2013 by Dee E. Fell
Revised Edition, copyright 2016 by Dee E. Fell
ISBN-13: 978-0692486955
All rights reserved
Published by Dee E. Fell
E-mail: Shinobidi46@aol.com
Manufactured in the United States of America

Dedicated to Bill for his love, enthusiasm, and support.
Also, in memory of an inspiring little poodle
whom I will forever lovingly hold in my heart.

CONTENTS

Introduction 4
Disclaimer 8
Poems:
    Lottery Winners 10
    Can't Recall 11
    Shinobi! Shinobi! 12
    Just Canned Peas 13
    There's a Devil in My Christmas Tree 14
    Keeper of the Bathroom 16
    Two Will Do 17
    Shop Cat 18
    More Than Meets the Eye 19
    Flying Ted 20
    X Marks the Spot 21
    Shop Cat Comes Home 22
    Not Even in a Dream 23
    Promises Are Made to be Kept 24
    Hey Little Ray! 25
    In and Out and Running About 26
    Taking Care of Business 27
    What's in a Name? 28
    ? In the Box 29
    Do Cats Go to Heaven? 30
    Sleepy Raiders 31
    It's Warm Inside 32
    Hair Balls 33
    Strange Little Duos 34
    Forever 35
Shinobi 36
Bart 42
Jessie 50
Ray 56
Teddy 62
Abbey 70
Family Photos 78
A Loving Glance 85
    * A Better Way.....AFTER READING POEMS AND SHORT STORIES, THIS FINAL CHAPTER IS TO SHARE SOME SAFETY AND HEALTH FACTORS I HAVE SINCE LEARNED TO TAKE BETTER CARE OF MY LITTLE FRIENDS 97

INTRODUCTION

  I woke up one morning and found myself to be the leader of the pack, having a female Brindle Boxer named Zeney; a male Golden Retriever, Max; and a smaller female we call Ginger who is a mixture of Golden Retriever and Brittany Spaniel; four cats and growing; and a ferret named Farrah Jo. We will find out later that she is a he, but we still call him Farrah Jo. Most of these animals are throw-away animals, which I adopted because ultimately, I could not say no to them.
  Before our animal family started to grow, I was enjoying my perfect world, which I considered to include myself, spouse, and children. This for me was the perfect scenario. No messy, noisy, time-consuming animals for us even though my sons' and husband's pleads were constant. Then it happened! A part of me died every time I turned away an animal my family begged me to keep. It started to hurt too much to say no. I weakened!
  As our animal family started to grow, so did my internal struggle. I fought with the overwhelming feeling of being out of control. I was upset and disappointed with myself for not being able to reject these animals as they undermined my harmonious lifestyle. With each new addition, I faced the fear of not being able to draw a line and set a limit. This was something I was always able to do in my life, and I was very good at it. Also, with this inability came the sensation of a draining strength from within. This was very scary to me and put me into an emotional tailspin. There were times this emotional turmoil was heightened to what I now describe as panic attacks. Still, to each new pet I could not say no even though there was a part of me screaming, "No, no, no, not another animal!" There was a part of me hurting even more to turn them away onto unknown destinies. My resistance was weakened against them as they entered and upset my perfect world. I started to see them as children who never grow up. Emotionally, it was like being on an amusement ride, going up and down. I wanted to get off, but I could not do it. I was compelled to ride it to the finish. I had a strong feeling there would be end results greater than I could imagine. This feeling of anticipation could be best described as standing in the dark at my own surprise party, knowing the lights were going to go on with the word "surprise" yelled. I just kept waiting for someone to turn on the lights.

INTRODUCTION

As I went completely with the positive feelings I had for these new foundlings, I was finally able to stop fighting with myself. I realized I had learned to be more trusting of my own instincts by taking a chance on this whole new kind of love. Love was the synergist as well as the victor of this internal struggle. Love replenished the strength I needed to overcome my greatest fears. I then had both the peace and strength to go with the good and the bad. I could go the distance in my now upside-down world. I found as my daily regimes turned into a nightmarish discord, love was again the common denominator. These animals made such an impact on our lives that things were never again the same.

It was a lot of work to keep up with them. I had plenty of trials and tribulations, but the salvaging factor was love.

Occasionally, there still is anguish in trying to maintain them, but the feelings of gratification I experience are more than a fair compensation.

The lessons in life that I have learned through them are priceless. Also, they have changed me for the better. They have all added to the family unit because they are family. My children have developed respect for nature through them, a sense of responsibility, and their realm of love has also been widened.

Through these pets, I have learned to be more sensitive to the needs of others besides those of my family. I have learned to give, give, and give. From this giving, I have learned to accept love back in return from all others. From so much giving, I became the vulnerable and needy one. I was ready to absorb any and all of the warmth from those who would cross my path. I have since developed a greater tolerance level for the helpless and needy. Relationships with friends, both old and new acquaintances, and other family memebers took on a deeper meaning. I have come to a better understanding and realization of the capacity of my love for all. For my family, there was always my total love and devotion while showing signs of eccentricity. There is now an extension of this love, expanding to encompass not only these precious pets but people I meet every day. By overcoming the fears that stagnated my emotional and spiritual growth, I have found myself on the horizon of a whole new world of love. I found

INTRODUCTION

myself becoming a more compassionate human being. "Surprise!" The lights were finally turned on!

A victory for me with the lessons I have learned! With a brand-new change in my outlook, I now handle things in life differently. While trusting my deepest instincts, I face things head-on as I take more chances.

I now know I can overcome the worst of obstacles if there is love, faith, and the persistence to do so. The experiences and conflicts I have endured through these animals have helped to make me a better-equipped person to accept and deal with my own recent bout of breast cancer. I have been through a lot, but life still looks better than ever! I emerged myself in a sea of love and surrounded myself with family and friends. I found it easy to open myself to them. Instinctively, I knew with love, faith, and the will to overcome, God would again see me through. I live each day with the small miracle I have encountered through the response of all those with whom I shared my physical and mental ordeals. The response of others to me during this battle with cancer was so overwhelmingly supportive. It was God's way of walking with me. I now know God will always be walking next to me with every step I take. I am glad I took that first big step forward with the help of my furry friends. Through them I have become a more emotionally open and giving person. Without them who knows what effect this devastating disease and its recurrence might have had on me both physically and psychologically?

I used to think it would be magical to be able to turn away an animal ever again. Needless to say, at this time in my life, I do not feel so weakened and disappointed with my inability to say no to any little friend who needs my help. The real magic is in what I have received from these lovable creatures. The real strength was in going with my instincts as I smothered within me the constant yelling of, "No, no, no, not another animal!" I am imprisoned by the love for these drifters, and it is more than alright to be so.

I feel like a candle, lit with warmth and love. Warmth lives in a spark, and these animals were my spark for that warmth and love to grow.

INTRODUCTION

    I sincerely dislike hearing these words . . . "They are just animals." If we let them, they are a key to open our hearts and let the love flow. Through them we can learn to touch and how to be touched. They were to me God's wake-up call.

Dee E. Fell

DISCLAIMER

The following is not intended to be professional advice. It contains subjects I have encountered as an animal lover. I share and also elaborate on some issues only to bring to light what you might need to know and want to research on your own as a responsible owner. Hopefully, you will find your own answers from credible sources and professionals.

May your love, care, and concern as a pet owner, be guided with the enlightenment needed in your quest to make a difference.

Please note that some of the enclosed information can become obsolete with new findings in veterinarian medicine and also animal care issues other than medical. I advise you to keep abreast of any and all information enclosed through media, etc. Do your research and consult with credible sources and professionals to confirm any and all found information.

Your vet is the professional and always consult him in reference to any health issues regarding the best care for your pet.

POEMS

LOTTERY WINNERS

There were six winners in all:
      One in the summer, one in the winter,
      One in the spring, and three in the fall.
Two were Shinobi and Jessie, both broken and bruised;
One was Ray, lost in the rain and no place to snooze;
The other was Bart, found in the trash;
And another, Ted, in a box with a gash;
The last was Shop Cat, abandoned and soon to be sick,
With very little savvy, staying alive was a trick.
All were found and taken home to be safe and sound;
Although two are demised, I really did try.
They all knew they were loved, had shelter,
And plenty of food,
With their own spaces, in my bed too.
Yes, my home became a little zoo,
But not for long did I brood . . .
I found I also was a winner 'cause I learned soon:
In their own way they loved me true!

CAN'T RECALL

From the table and back,
Now, here I sit.
What happened to my snack?
I must have finished it,
But can't quite recall.
I don't remember the taste at all!
Then reaching up, a little white paw;
There between her legs, crumbs I saw,
And I know this snack to the floor . . .
Just didn't fall!
Maybe Jessie can recall?

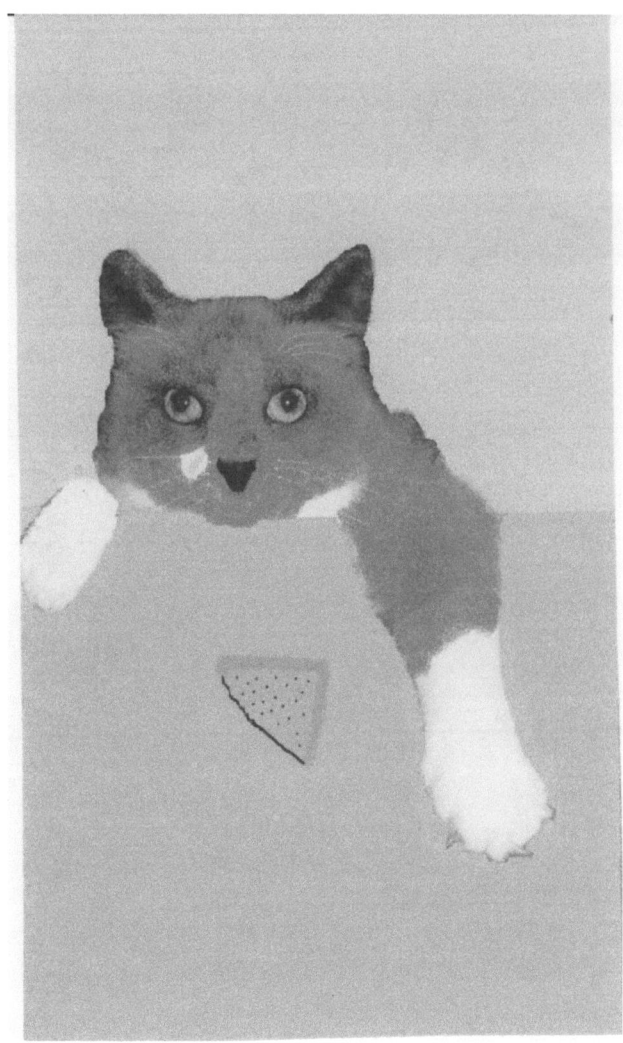

SHINOBI! SHINOBI!

Shinobi! Shinobi!
Where are you?
I've called your name till blue,
And in all your hiding places I've checked too.
Are you mad at me?
What have I done?
Or all just to tease?
Shinobi, Shinobi this isn't fun!
Now, dawn has come,
And still no Shinobi.
Where can she be?
There she is looking in at me!
And at my feet a killed hunt she leaves . . .
I thank her for thinking of me:
For her bowl was empty,
And now both of us she feeds.

JUST CANNED PEAS

Teddy is so hard to please,
Dry food in his bowl does not appease.
With each grinding can-opener sound,
Hopes of new treats to be found.
There he is at my feet,
Crying, "Give me something to eat!"
Not every can a fishy dish,
Sometimes corn, carrots, and peas,
But still here comes Ted with great speed!
He thinks I'm just a nasty tease,
Taking swats at my knees,
I now start to bleed,
And he just cries, "Feed me!"

THERE'S A DEVIL IN MY
CHRISTMAS TREE

Tree decorated with strings of colorful shining lights,
Golden garland going round and round,
Oh, what a sight!
Each fragile ornament and ball so meticulously hung;
Shining lights bouncing off all, making this tree even more bright,
And a little silver tinsel added just for fun.
Finally, atop favorite angel, gently placed, just right,
Standing back and saying, "Well done . . ."
Before my eyes such disbelief!
"Oh, no God!" with Bart it is wreathed,
He is playing cat and mouse in my Christmas tree,
Scampering recklessly, bringing treasured trinkets to my knees.
Tree bent, swaying side to side, building speed;
As I scream, he takes no heed.
From hugged branches he stretches paws,
Swatting at swinging ornaments and balls . . .
So meticulously hung.
Now wearing silver tinsel, added just for fun,
A flight ever so fast to the full six-foot height he runs,
Only to find atop . . . not a mouse at all,
Just favorite angel, gently placed, just right,
Now dancing to a fall . . .
And as if too a fallen angel, to the floor he jumps,
Taking strings of colorful shining lights,
And silver tinsel now in clumps,
Leaving my Christmas tree a bare and naked sight,
Standing back and crying, "I swear not fair."
"As if just for you, placed there!"

KEEPER OF THE BATHROOM

It's a dirty job, but someone has to do it!
Is it a morality issue,
Watching every sheet of tissue,
So none is wasted here?
Or is it the fanciful tune that keeps him this near?
As it spins and flutters on its holder,
Becoming bolder and bolder,
Setting free playful paws,
Swatting and batting harder and harder,
At what he thinks,
A falling bird or tottering ball . . .
Maybe none of this at all.
Perhaps just counting each refreshing flush,
Keeping bathroom smells shampoo-sweet,
An absolute must.
Also, that all are washed in the tub from head to feet,
Or is it the splutter of fun-filled flushes,
That stir thoughts of a fish in defeat,
From frisky paws that have taken a many catch
Down by the creek?
Or is it his dewy fur, as if in a simple summer's rain,
From this morning's showers' moistened heat?
Maybe none of this at all, for now he strains
To watch shaved beards and all loosened hairs,
So none will be left here,
Keeping everything just fair?
As teeth are scrubbed,
Watches toothpaste squeezed from the rear,
So there will be plenty to spare?
Still, maybe none of all this so-called fun . . .
Perhaps just watching and waiting,
For a little of morning's sun!

TWO WILL DO

When the world seems like a zoo,
I sit and sigh.
To find a little solitude would do.
Just before I started to cry,
A head nudges into mine,
And a warm little body at my side . . .
He has come to my rescue.
There couldn't be a more perfect time,
As if baby Bart knew,
Or maybe, he's just looking for a little love too!

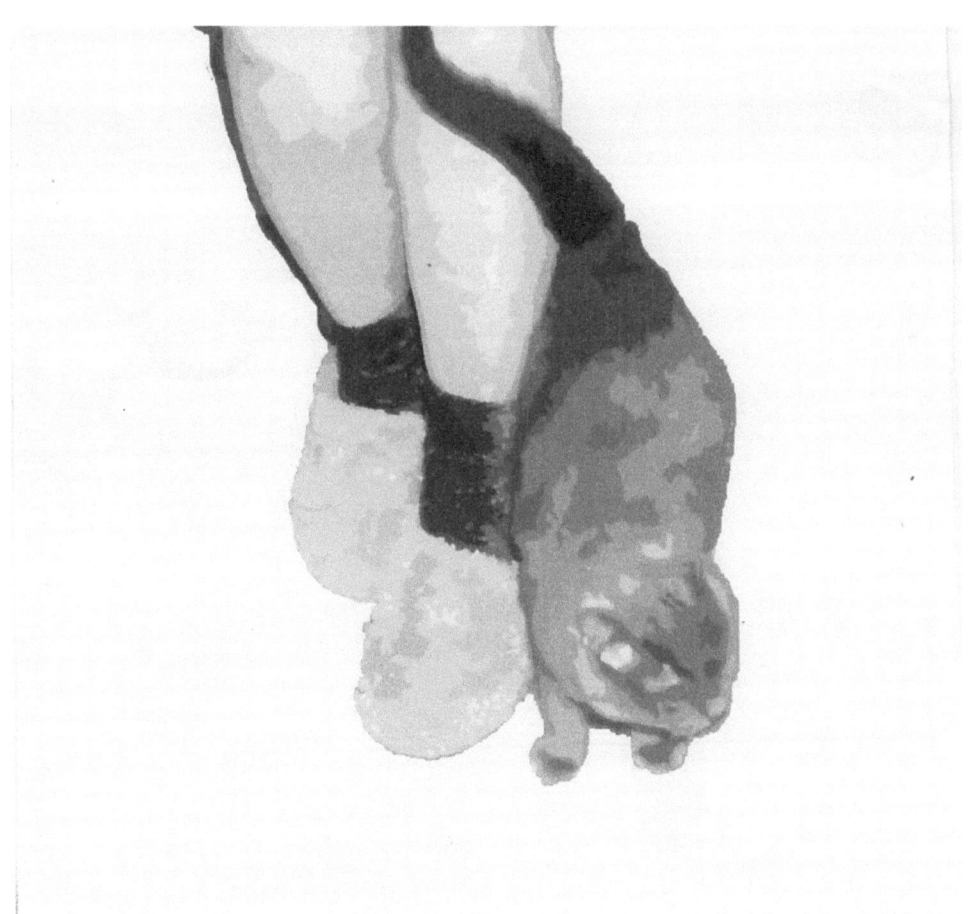

SHOP CAT

She was found just hanging around,
So skinny and small,
Black with tiny white paws,
So to our crazy and hectic office she did go,
Where her bowls would overflow,
And upon desks to nap,
She was called our Shop Cat.
In the office she did remain;
There she stayed night and day,
Till sick she became.
To the vet's we made a trip,
And he reassured us we were not to blame,
"Because from a previous bug bite she is sick."
For a long time she stayed with him,
And now healthy and no longer thin,
Food is her main focus,
Believe this 'cause anyone can see . . .
She's our fat lady in this circus.

MORE THAN MEETS THE EYE

Jessie girl sitting on top my dishwasher,
I know not always looking for food,
Watching me stack plates and saucers,
And a dirty pot from tonight's stew.
As I swear, "I'll never get done . . ."
She thinks, "Oh, what fun!"

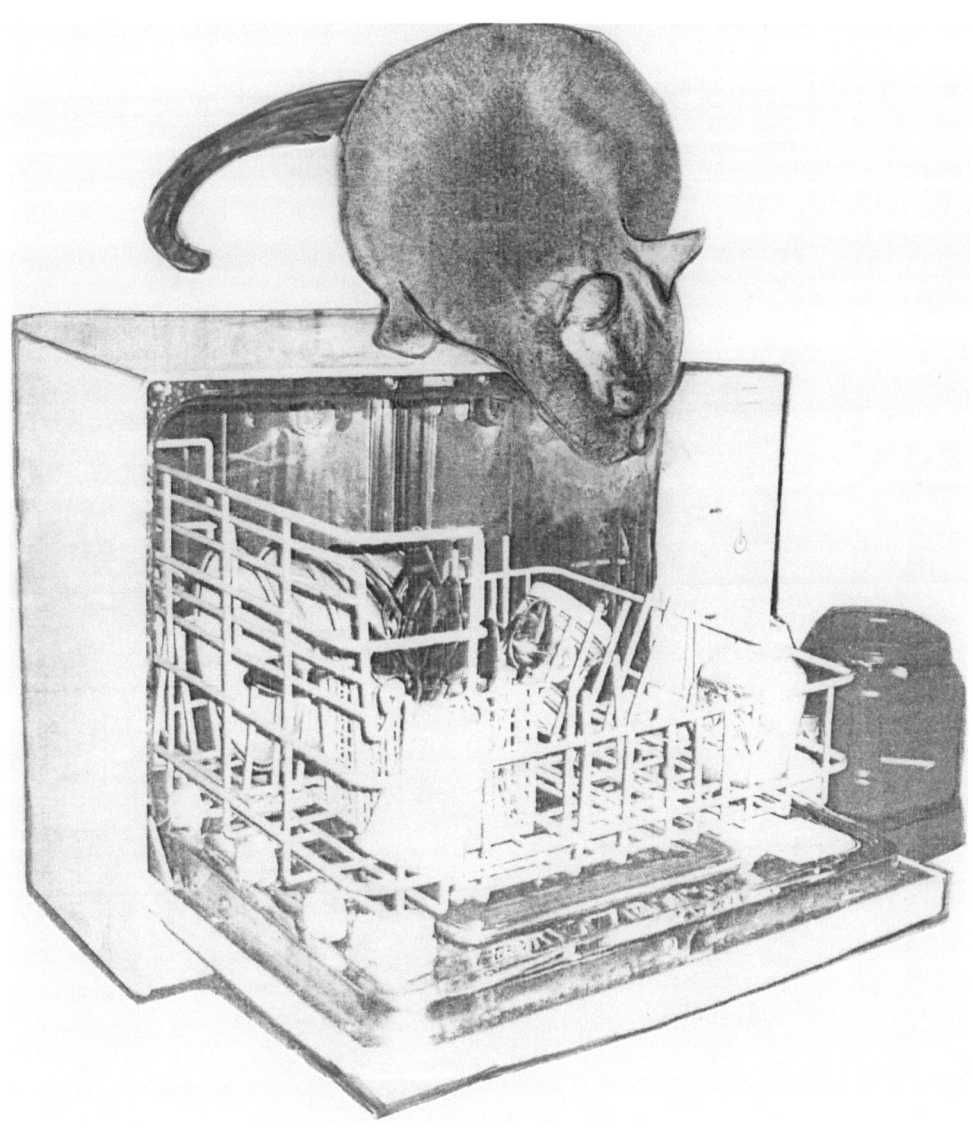

FLYING TED

What the heck was that?
Perhaps a bat,
No, just my cat,
So wound up and nothing better to do,
Running through,
From door to door,
And bouncing off the floor.
Kicked up scatter rugs hitting me in the knees,
Boy, oh boy, is he building up speed,
I can feel the breeze!
Then as he goes by, a jump so high,
Oh my, oh my, he can fly!
Front legs strecthed with extended claws,
Watch out one and all,
He's coming in for a fall!

X MARKS THE SPOT

In this chair I'll save your place,
Keeping it all so warm and safe.
I'll make like an X,
With forepaws crossed and
Bent to my chest,
Keeping it only your spot,
Just as a marker found on top.

SHOP CAT COMES HOME

An office was no fit place we did decide,
For such a sweet and loving cat to reside,
So we brought her home, our Shop Cat dear,
Only to find our Shinobi became one big fear.
Shop Cat had such a knack to stalk and chase,
As if to steal our Shinobi's place.
It took a while, but Shop Cat did learn:
Though Shinobi is first, everyone gets their turn.
This lesson did not come easily because I had to be firm . . .
Now Shop Cat is our loving pet,
Because she now knows who is really the threat!

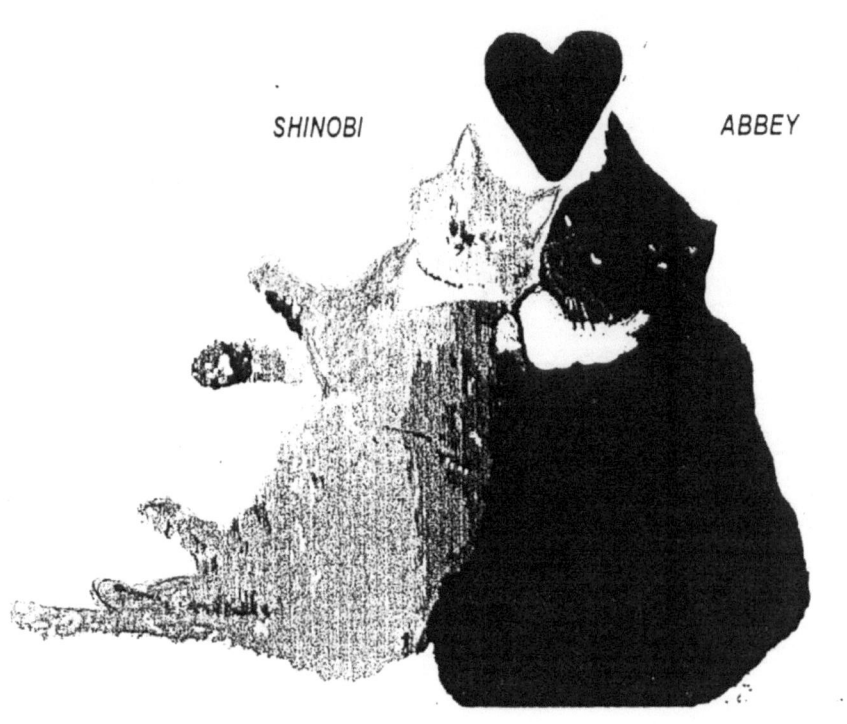

NOT EVEN IN A DREAM

When I go to sleep at night,
I dream of them as me,
Saying nice little things,
Like thank you and please,
And a God bless you if you sneeze.
Then in my dream I realize,
None of these things they would ever do,
No more than they could cook stew,
And I think you know why . . .
For within each one of them resides,
The only dish that they can brew,
Serving it piled high,
And calling it, "Attitude!"

PROMISES ARE MADE TO BE KEPT

Just sitting and watching,
Such playful fish bouncing about,
Now, I'm not feeling quite so bored.
Maybe just one little slap on the snout,
I promise nothing more.
Little fish under me so prissy;
In your glass house so protected and safe.
Just a big tease swishing between bubbles so fizzy,
With such a fast pace,
Making me feel ever so dizzy,
First coming to the top,
Then quickly down to peak beneath.
Busy, busy fishy swimming around that sunken rock,
Remember, I am the one with teeth.
Perhaps just looking for an escape?
Now, I know truly it is you that is so bored!
I can help without hook or bait,
I promise nothing more,
Than the desire to set you free,
And with no one really keeping score,
This little white paw building up speed,
And giving a quick lash,
With a little splash,
Has both of us freed.
Now, neither of us so bored,
Oh yes, and with such a good taste in me,
I'll just sit and watch . . .
Promising to help some more!

HEY LITTLE RAY

As little Ray revives from a morning nap,
He squints and stretches,
And upon his back, allows only one little pat,
Any more than that,
He'll return your concern with a playful slap.

IN AND OUT AND RUNNING ABOUT

So many cat tails put me in a spin,
Nerves wearing thin,
I don't know who's out or who's in.
Try as I may to keep them to stay,
Still, some run by me and walk away.
So for them cans of food:
White Ocean Fish, Salmon, and Tuna too,
Whatever it takes to keep them in will do.
To my dismay with fishy breaths,
Tails and heads held high,
Still, they walk away,
As though some secret mission to abide.
And I fret if they will be here for another day,
Because all I can think of is little Ray;
He slept next to me, ate his food, and played,
And still he walked away,
But he never made it back to spend that other day.
My heart skips a beat!
Here they come as though in defeat,
Shinobi, Bart, and Ted,
Now in my bed to stay,
And with fishy breaths as they sleep,
Is a gift to me that this day they didn't stray.

TAKING CARE OF BUSINESS

Ray after Jessie, Jessie after Bart,
Shinobi just looking on and not taking any part,
Jessie jumps in pan,
Ray and Bart in a frozen stance,
She scratches in litter as to signal, she's done,
And hops from her pan to resume the fun,
Ray after Jessie, Jessie after Bart,
Shinobi just looking on and not taking any part.

WHAT'S IN A NAME?

Shop Cat gained a lot of fame,
By such a silly name,
But to call Shop Cat, Shop Cat, Shop Cat,
Just doesn't have a ring,
We had to think of something that would sing,
Abbey came to mind,
Yes, Abbey sounds mighty fine,
Abbey, Abbey, Abbey rings true,
Now, if she'd just come, it will do!

? IN THE BOX

Such a little stinker is Ted,
Done eating, now wishes to play instead.
He thinks, "Where is Ray, that silly clown?"
"I'll just hide and wait around!"
Ted sees Ray and pulls him down.
An empty box, the only stake,
Now for them both there is no escape,
As they go round and round,
Our stinker and clown.
No hissing or thrashing about,
Not even one little sound,
Nor biting mouth,
Just good clean fun.
And when they are done,
He that is least tired has won,
The empty box is his to keep,
And now in it, he sleeps and sleeps.

DO CATS GO TO HEAVEN?

I'm told all felines have lives of nine,
And then where do they go?
I'd like to know.
Do cats go to heaven?
Or maybe, they don't go at all,
      For as I can recall,
        After all those falls,
        Lives 9, 8, 7,
        Still he's not in heaven.
        And then he fell through the floor,
        And got caught in our door,
        Can't be sure,
        6, 5, 4,
        Seems like much more.
And still he's running in the sun;
 For him no pearly white gates,
Having all this fun!
Heaven can wait,
Feeling ever so fine,
A saint must be sent for speed!
He can't make up his mind,
Is it 9×9 to the nth degree?

SLEEPY RAIDERS

Jessie sleeps ever so vigilantly at my son's feet.
Both in dreams so sound,
I wonder what they could be . . .
Is Jessie's of running through our grounds,
Hiding, hunting, and climbing trees?
Is his of . . . I wish it could be me?
For not on either face a frown.
Does she lie there all comfy, cozy
As if to share this slumber sleep?
Or is all just a desperate feat,
Waiting for him to get up and eat?
She poses feline head so sweetly upon both front paws,
And teeth not giving even one little gnaw,
Curled just like a fuzzy gray ball,
Small body all so bent,
And well-groomed tail the same.
Is she dreaming of time well spent?
Or is it of great fame,
Knowing she will never be tamed?
I guess none of these . . . 'cause there's
Jessie nibbling at his knee!
As if not to be noticed as an angry plea,
Crying inside . . . "Get up and feed me!"

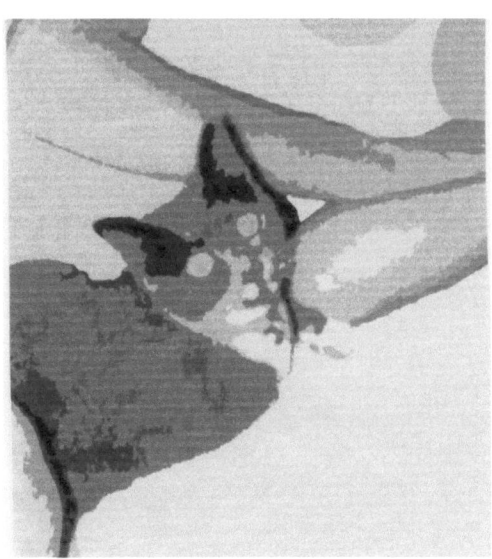

IT'S WARM INSIDE

Wood stove burning hot,
In front, Jessie sleeps lying stretched on one side,
Any closer she'd be on top.
Peeping from behind dozing eyes,
She thinks she's in the summer sun,
Yawns and rolls to the other side,
As if to cook till done,
And as I watch, in us both the warmth resides.

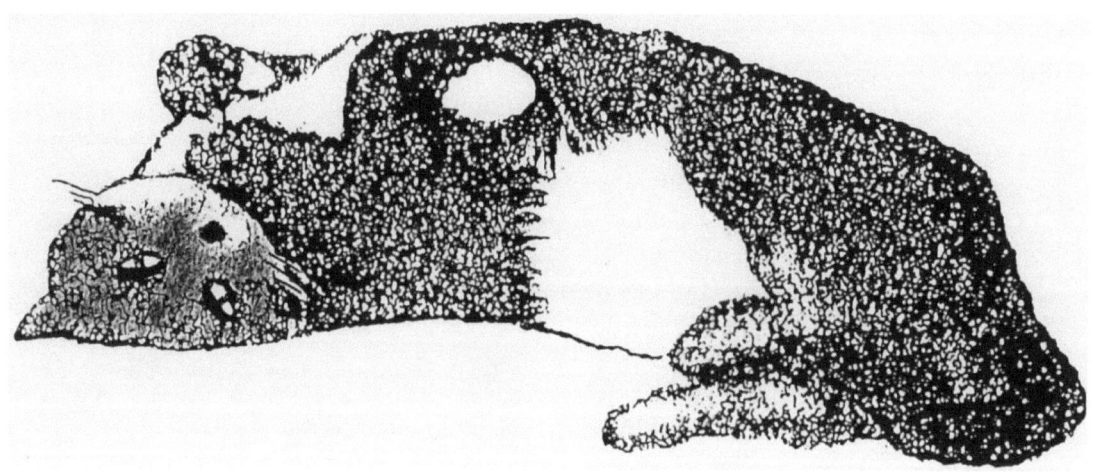

HAIR BALLS

Oh, to be a cat,
Wearing all this hair!
I sometimes feel so trapped;
I keep licking spots till almost bare,
And hair mixed with food,
Next day causing me to spew,
And funky looking little balls I find . . .
Which I hopelessly and tiresomely say,
"All are still mine!"

STRANGE LITTLE DUOS

Shinobi and Bart are a duo,
Abbey and Ted are also.
Shinobi and Bart rub noses;
While Abbey and Ted exchange rapid swats in fighting poses.
Ted is full of spirit,
And Abbey does not fear it.
Now, a fight between Ted and Bart will last all day once they start.
While Abbey has learned to be sweet,
When left with Shinobi, who insists on nothing but peace.
If Ted is with Shinobi, she will run away.
Yet, if Bart is with Abbey, she is the one to stay?

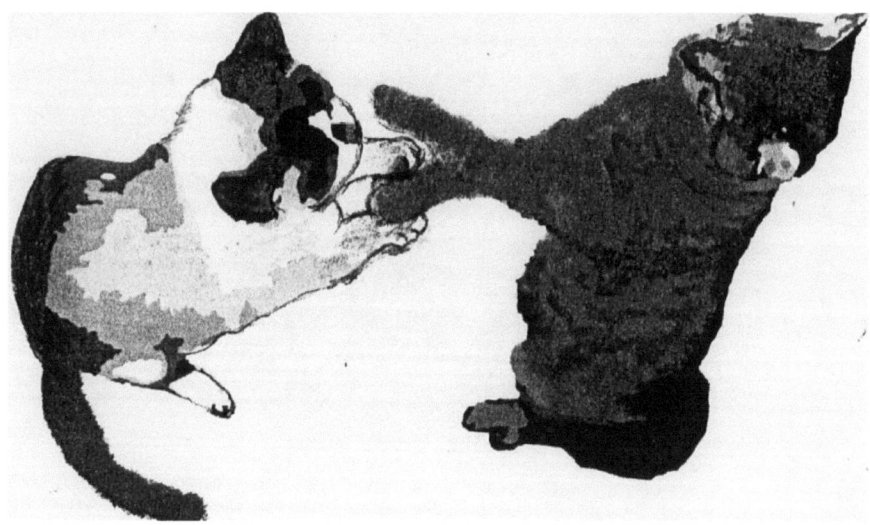

FOREVER

FOR ALL THE PETS WHO HAVE CROSSED OVER

Oh why, oh why, is my best friend gone? Just yesterday he was here to rub and hug, pet and love. Only with him did I share feelings . . . with others I would not dare. He loved me always, trusted me forever, and needed me the most. He shared it all and gave his best. As I look around, "Never again," I swear. Now, all that is left are old used toys, empty bowls, and yes . . . some loose hair, which I once rubbed and hugged, petted and loved.

So hard to bear, for in my heart he has touched a place as no one could. Now, this loss and void leaves such a heaviness in my chest. Oh why, oh why, did he have to go?

God's little creatures are so hard to lay to rest. For them we grieve the most, yet no one taught us how. Does he know the love I had for him and always will? I don't know how to feel! It is all so unfair, and I am angry . . . "He is not here!"

This broken heart is so hard to heal. As I fumble with and grasp for thoughts of comfort, I realize . . . once they leave here, they are not just in the ground under a tree. Their little souls made speed unto God's loving arms. In his love, He created them for me to rub and hug, pet and love in any place. This is why they will wait in a place called Forever.

Dear God, thank you for all of your furry little gifts who made each day in this world a better place. Because you know heaven would not be home without them, keep these furry gifts tightly wrapped in your loving arms. When we are rejoined, I will unwrap each one in celebration of our life together again, rubbing and hugging, petting and loving all in this happy place called Forever. Lastly, until we meet again, I send my deepest love to them because I was their only friend.

SHINOBI

SHINOBI

It was a fall night, Friday, October 21, 1988, to be exact when I was surprised by a tiny orange ball of fur. It followed me to the fence and bounced off the gate. It then quickly ran back into one of our open sheds. It was a baby female kitten with an injured mouth, and it looked as if she had been kicked in it. The little ball of fur took up residency in our shed. I returned with a box of some rags for her. Also, I made sure she had plenty of food and water for the night. I was not quick to bring her into the house for more than one reason. The first three reasons were the dogs we had. Another reason was our sixteen-year-old male cat, Frenchie. Lastly, I did not want or need another friend.

That night I questioned my oldest son about the fuzzy orange ball now living in our shed. He tried to play innocent, but he gave himself away when he said he did not know anything about the girl kitten. Upon further questioning him, he confessed he had put her in our yard for lack of a better idea as to what to do with her.

He found her in the parking lot of a fast-food restaurant on the other side of town. She was six to eight weeks old and looking for food with an injured mouth on this parking lot. This was too much for my son to endure since he is an animal lover himself. He decided he could do better for her even if it meant starting her out in our backyard. This was a smart move on his part because the next day I checked her every fifteen minutes. My last visit to check her was very upsetting because she was shivering. I could not stand it anymore. I then brought her into the house to pet and cuddle, to keep and love, and for my youngest son to call Shinobi. She is now about seven years old. Her mouth is fine. She is part of the gang and enjoys our home better than we do.

Sometimes, when we call … "Shinobi," it sounds like "Snowbe," which seems to fit her because of the beautiful, fleecy white fur she carries on her chest. It looks like a patch of untouched snow you want to caress in hopes of forming the perfect snowball.

On her front right paw is a round dot of reddish-brown fur. This being the only spot of color on any of her white-tipped paws, I have to call it a beauty mark. Her orange fur is so silky; sometimes, I feel as though she will slip right out of my hands.

SHINOBI

Some of my most endearing memories of her were when she was a kitten, and she made herself so at home. She took right over as if she owned the place. I remember the first Christmas after we found her. As I was feverishly working to remove Christmas decorations from their storage boxes, she was jumping in and out of the boxes, onto a shelf, and then up the stairs. Then she would start all over again, beginning with the boxes. She made me feel in her way. I wanted to step back and take a seat until she was done with her run.

That Christmas I had to replace the glass Christmas balls on the lower branches of our tree with nylon ones. She enjoyed playing with them, and I could not keep up with her. First, she would swat at them until they fell off the tree. If this did not break them, she would proceed paddling them around the room with her little white paws until they either broke or got lost under a piece of furniture.

I remember another thing she did as a kitten: She thought it was so neat to just come in and out of the windows as I opened them to clean. It was a thrill for her not to be detained by any closed-doors or windows.

When we first found her, she tried to play with Frenchie, our elderly male cat. I tried to keep Shinobi from stressing him out because of his age. All Frenchie really wanted was to eat and sleep. He lived for another year after we found our baby Shinobi. When he became sick, Shinobi knew something was wrong; she would lie next to him and lick him.

I pampered her as a baby. Maybe I did this because she was our first female kitten. It still shows because sometimes she reminds me of a prima donna. She will only let you pet her when she is ready for some bonding. I have to pet her with very soft strokes while making sure not to pet her around the neck. There is, however, always one place she loves to have rubbed and that is her little pink nose. She got used to this when she was a kitten. I would feel her nose to see if it was warm or dry. I do not know how medically correct this was. It was my way of checking to see if she was getting sick from any of the needles she received from the vet earlier in the day. She always seemed to enjoy this ritual.

SHINOBI

　　　Something else she enjoys is to use the extra large dog house we have for our Golden Retriever. She has been doing this since she was little and is the only one of our cats who does it. It looks so funny to see her sitting in this large dog house, which the dogs do not even use because they are indoor pets.
　　　Presently speaking, Shinobi is a peacemaker. She refuses to be involved in any entangled episodes with the other felines whom we now have living with us. She is very gentle, and if you ask her for kisses, she will give your nose or cheek a nice lick. Shinobi is timid and easily intimidated. She is especially intimidated by other female cats even if they are smaller than she is. The reaction she has is as though her style were being severely cramped. She will lose her personality and take flight.
　　　Shinobi is also very musical. She sings her meows, and you know how badly she wants something by the notes she will hit. If she goes off key, she is just feeling the need to whine. I have also discovered that she loves to listen to my music boxes. When she hears one playing, she will come running to join in with her meows while she also rubs her head back and forth on my leg. I even find myself singing her name. She seems to respond faster if I sing … " Shinobi" in high-pitched notes. Her ears turn to listen as though they were little radars.
　　　I believe she has Abyssinian in her somewhat by her appearance but mostly because of her musical inclinations. In any event, because of her musical talents, she is a prima donna in the true sense of the word.

SHINOBI

SHINOBI

BART

BART

It was a Tuesday night, July 10, 1990, when my sons came home with a second newfound friend. It was almost two years after finding Shinobi. This was a gray male kitten whom they found crying in a dumpster in the back of the mall. He was about three-and-a-half months old. He weighed only four pounds and was pigeon-toed. His sister or brother was also in the dumpster but was dead. He cried all the way home and into my arms.

Upon receiving him and knowing where he had been just minutes before, I decided to bathe him. As I emerged him into his bathwater, I spoke to him to reassure him he was safe and loved. He stopped crying to listen to me, and he has not cried like that since.

There was no controlling what was becoming a situation here at home. At one time in my life, I was so good at saying the word "no." Now, it is an impossible dream to be able to say it ever again when it comes to these furry, helpless creatures. Finally, I stopped fighting with myself and named him Bart! I overcame my disappointment in not being able to say no to another animal because I have come to love these needy foundlings all too much.

I can remember when I really fell in love with this small gray fellow who is a Russian Blue. He jumped off the top of the couch and limped to his litter pan. For the first couple of months, he lived on top of the couch to keep out of the way of our dogs. One of the dogs must have been a little rough with him in my absence. It was both sad and precious how this little guy struggled to use his pan like such a good boy. He had no medical problem from the limp as it was very short-lived.

I recall his first Christmas with us as I finished painstakingly trimming the tree. It was a work of art. I then proudly stood back to admire this piece of art. There in the middle of it, I found Bart! He raced to its top as if in a hunt for a flying bird or a scampering mouse. I almost died right there where I stood. The tree swayed from side to side, and things only got worse as he removed himself from it. He did all but totally destroy our Christmas tree. I was relieved to be able to salvage it with some more work. After that exploration of the tree, Bart never ventured off into it again. I thank God for that and for baby Bart.

BART

Bart is now a large gray cat weighing in at thirteen pounds. He shows all the characteristics of a Russian Blue from his thick, plush coat to his pinkish-purple paw pads. He has an expression on his face that makes him look as if he were smiling.

Bart and Shinobi are the best of friends. They greet each other by touching noses. When they were smaller, I could put them both into the same traveling kennel, which I used for our trips to the animal hospital. There was no trouble between them. I would even say that they actually enjoyed being together. I do know for a fact they give each other moral support. On one of our more recent trips to the vet, they were both on the examination table with only two feet between them. This was not good enough for Bart. He stretched his agile, gray body over to Shinobi until he felt safe and secure in her orange fur. While they cuddled waiting for the doctor, they tucked their little front legs under their breasts. They searched the room with wide, watchful eyes and focused on my every move. They made my heart drop. Immediately, I went to their rescue to caress them and softly speak to them as we all waited for the doctor. When he first came into the room, he even remarked how cute they looked cuddled together. Each was there for the other to make stronger for the unknown.

As hard as I try to keep Bart and Shinobi in, I am a failure. I remember their first attempt to stay outside as they ran out and under the deck. I would stay there by the deck sometimes for a half-hour waiting and calling for them. Eventually, I realized it was hopeless; I could not keep doing this every day.

Bart is the hardest to keep in the house because of his unique efforts to have the freedom of the outdoors. He meows at every door available to him. He plucks at all our screen windows with his claws as if he were playing the harp. When opening the door from the outside, we will sometimes find Bart hanging onto the inside of it as though he were a stretched animal hide.

Also, Bart is learning from watching us how to work door knobs and latches with his front paws. I was home alone working in the kitchen, and I heard the door knob to my son's room turning. I froze; then I realized it was Bart on the other side, turning the knob back and forth with his pinkish-purple paw pads. Earlier, when my youngest son closed his bedroom door, he forgot Bart

BART

was still in the bedroom. I know to watch so he is not locked in a room again. Bart can only open or close doors that are not completely shut. He will push and pull on them to suit his needs. Also, he knows that all he has to do for the latch on the storm door is to hit it with his paw. When Bart knows he is defeated after standing on his hind legs and smacking at the storm door latch, he will then hit my hand and cry. He could not make it clearer that he wants me to open the door for him. He certainly seems to understand the mechanics of opening and closing doors. It is also obvioius how very hard he works at it.

When Bart wants to come in, he also has a unique coping technique for what he feels is a silly and unnecessary barrier. He will stand on his hind legs and rapidly move his front paws up and down on our glass patio door. These sounds are identical to the sounds of a window being cleaned with a squeegee. When we hear this noise, we know it can only be our Bart.

Bart reminds me of a miniature man when standing on his hind legs with such agility. I always did say that the trouble with cats— or I should say that the most exciting thing about cats is how they think they are human. Maybe one day after enough practice, he will be my pigeon-toed little doorman in his plush gray suit as he opens and closes doors for me.

Also, Bart is the one most likely to greet you on the walkway to our house. He will almost trip you for attention as he throws his body in front of you, taking a horizontal position on his back. He will stay there that way until you pet him on his stomach.

Shinobi is runner-up for the best greeter. She will also roll over on the walkway for you to pet her belly, but she is too ladylike to try to trip you.

Lately, when I find Bart outside, he blinks his large eyes at me. It is as though his eyelids were moving in slow motion. He projects a look so captivating and hard to describe. His face portrays a look of animation. You are made to think someone is whispering a lullaby in his ear as his eyes swell with slumber. This projects an expression of serenity on his face that is not of our world. He radiates with the peace and contentment of being outdoors because he is in perfect harmony with life. He is in his natural environment, and I call it "Bart's World."

BART

One night while in our hot tub, I looked up only to see Bart peering down at me from the overhead trellis. He was watching as if he were wishing he could join me. He wanted to see what fun was to be found in this. Another time when I ventured out into "Bart's World" to retrieve something from my car on the driveway, I looked over my right shoulder, and there was Bart on top of my husband's station wagon. He was reclining, propped by the car rack. He came out of nowhere to make a mystical appearance as he gave me that animated blink again.

He patrols our grounds, leaving nothing unturned. When you are outside, he will always find you. He will come to you for affection and, of course, out of curiosity. Bart thoroughly enjoys you being outside and sharing with him what he knows to be his world. With your company, he then has the best of both worlds ... his and yours.

I even had company call me later at night to thank me for a nice time and say, "I really like that gray cat." "He followed us all day." "He's neat!"

Bart is like a little angel outside as he watches over your shoulder wherever you go. When he is indoors, however, he is our little devil.

BART

BART

BART

JESSIE

JESSIE

I am introduced to our third newly found cat Sunday, May 5, 1991, around 10:30 p.m. It is my oldest son's 21st birthday. He explains to me how he found this small gray and white female cat in front of his friend's home. She was in the gutter crying and looking for food and shelter. His friend's mother told him that she would take her in, but she already has a pet. She is very concerned and worried about this skinny and frail animal. When she finds out my son is going to take her, she is very pleased and relieved. My son has also learned that earlier in the day children were going door to door with this little cat trying to sell her for three dollars.

This story upsets me even more as I look at this gray and white bundle and see something is wrong. She is very slender, especially at the hips. Her head looks too large for her body, which makes her beautiful yellowish-green eyes seem even bigger. In spite of her size, we will later find out from the vet that she is already about ten months old. From the back, as she sits, she is all gray and resembles a mouse with a long, matching gray tail. Later, I also find a crimp in the tip of that same long gray tail.

She has been on the streets all of her life and is undernourished. I fed her well and took her to the animal hospital. Our vet checks all of our newfound friends, especially for Feline Leukemia. If they are negative for Feline Leukemia, they then receive their vaccinations and are either spayed or neutered. Our newest friend followed this same agenda. When I took her to be spayed, I also asked the vet to examine her for a limp, which I just noticed. When I returned to pick her up from her operation, he informed me that he took x-rays.

The x-rays show she had a broken hip, and it healed on its own. It is obvious she was in some sort of an accident. This explains a lot and the crimp in the tip of her tail.

After she returned home, I watched her as we cuddled. I could have left her in the hospital a little longer, but I felt better having her close to me even though our vet has a staff around the clock. When my pets are in the animal hospital, I know they are safe because there will always be a staff there to observe them.

JESSIE

In the days to come, she started to have trouble keeping food in her stomach and problems with her bowels. After another trip to the hospital to have her bowels cleaned, I learned she needs special medication for the rest of her life. This medical issue is due to her accident prior to finding her. The medicine she needs is a capsule, which I have to force her to swallow. In order to do this, I have to keep her wrapped in a towel from the neck down to restrain her as I try to get the capsule to the back of her mouth without gagging her. I then gently rub her throat and blow into her nose to get her to swallow. I do not know which one of us hated this more. On one of these occasions, the capsule burst in her mouth, and she became sick and upset. She curled up alone next to our water heater all that night and all the next day. It seemed the cure was worse than the illness. There soon was a revision of this procedure, making it a better and more successful way for me to handle her medical problem. In addition, she gets a little treat afterwards.

She is congenial with all except Shinobi. Naturally, she is able to intimidate our prima donna because Jessie is a little, rough, and tough cat. She became this way by having to fend for herself for such a long time on the streets. She reminds me of a little cowgirl because of her tomboyish ways, and her coloring makes me think of a pony. I guess this is why I call her Jessie. This name seems to fit our little cowgirl.

Jessie knows she can upset Shinobi. This is so comical to me because Shinobi is larger than Jessie is. Their interactions have nothing to do with size or strength. One might even be convinced that Jessie's attempted attacks on Shinobi are not initiated by any real primal instincts but rather by a difference in personalities. I witness a head game each time they meet.

Jessie likes to sleep with my youngest son while waiting for him to get a midnight snack. She is always looking for food. Perhaps this is because of her medical problem. We do our best to accommodate her by buying and serving her a variety of cat foods, which we know she enjoys. She still has an appetite for people food from her earlier days on the streets.

JESSIE

Jessie still has some problems and sleeps on top of my son's fish tank to feel the warmth from the lights. She finds the heat soothing, and I am sure she has had more than one pleasant dream about the fish below her. Jessie also likes to sleep in front of our woodstove on cold winter nights, and she is so cozy there.

The vet told me that there was an operation for her hip, but we could not put her through this without first seeing how she was coping with her other medical problem. I kept an envelope with her name on it to save any extra money in for this operation.

I always had hope for her getting this operation so she would be a perfectly healthy cat. It never happened. We had to have her put to sleep, Friday, March 25, 1994. It was the humane thing to do. The problems with her bowels got worse, and she was not going to get better. She lost her quality of life. I know she had almost three good years with us even with her bad days. She had fun-filled days running in the sun. In addition, she learned to play and purr. After my son found her, she did not do either of these for quite a while. A cat's purr is not always a sign of a positive feeling; however, I knew she was happy because she purred while also playing.

When I think of her, I have many loving memories. She would jump off my son's fish tank and jump up onto my lap to be with me for hours as I watched TV and petted her. Due to her size, her biggest catch was usually a cricket. One day she brought me a live baby mouse. It was the smallest mouse I had ever seen. She was so proud of it. I let it go, of course, and she seemed a little disappointed in me for doing so. Whenever I took her by surprise, she purred, "Hmmmmm?" This cute, entertaining sound, as if to ask what I wanted, will be a sweet memory of her forever.

I often wonder what would have happened to her without us because of all her problems. I am thankful my son brought her home.

Her body did catch up with the size of her head, but she still was very small, especially for her age. For this reason, I always kept a bell on her safety collar so I could hear where she was at all times. I would call her, and she would come jumping through the grass to me with her tiny bell ringing, "Jessie girl, Jessie girl."

JESSIE

JESSIE

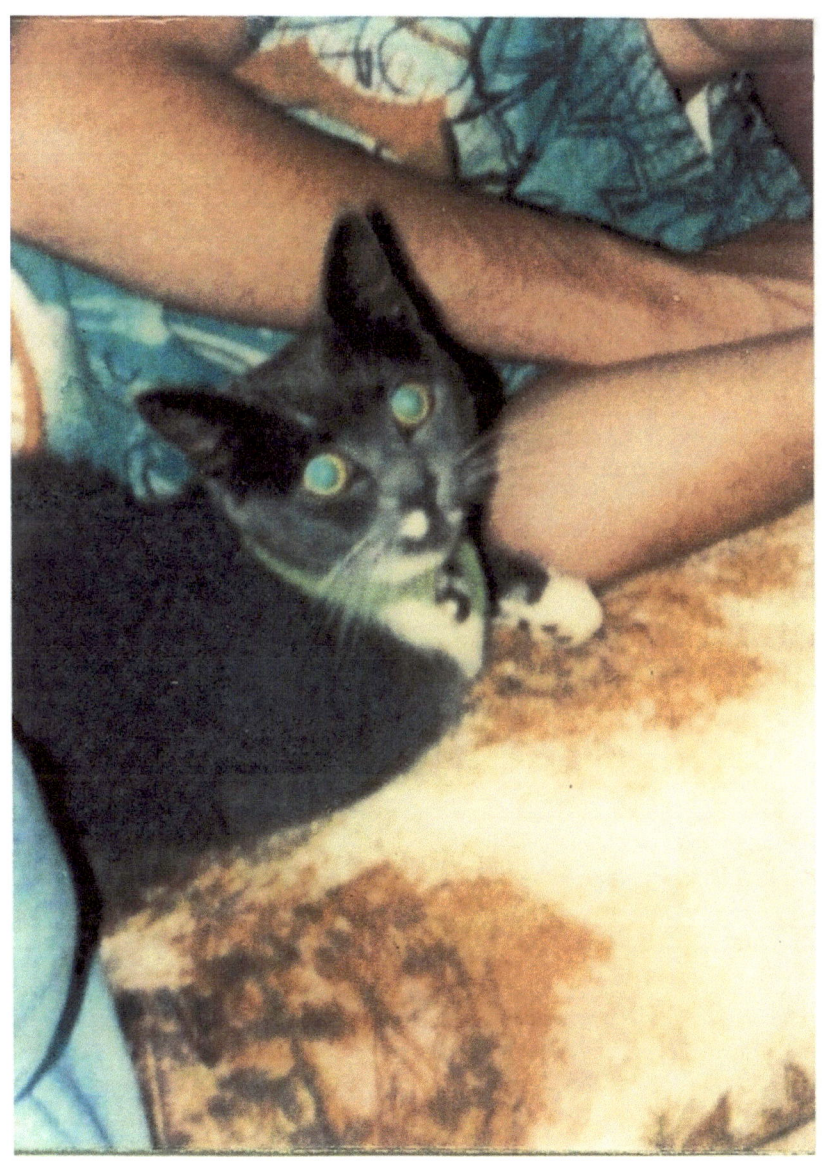

RAY

RAY

Our fourth cat came to us by way of my husband's office. There was a thunderstorm, and he ran into the office for shelter. They know just where to go! It was a Thursday, October 24, 1991, when my oldest son brought him home to me. He knew just where to bring him! Our new friend is so affectionate, and when he was in the office, he would run after everyone looking for love. Upon seeing him, I said, "Let's keep him."

He is a ten to twelve-month-old, rust and creamy beige tabby. His eyes are bright yellow and compliment his creamy beige stripes. They are large and almond-shaped with white fur outlining them as if they were done with white eyeliner makeup. His paws, having that same beautiful shade of beige, are large and look overstuffed, resembling the paws of a soft toy animal. They make me want to hold them and cuddle them forever. He is almost dear enough to agree to this. He loves to lie on your chest or under your arm, and he cannot get close enough. We all love him. Our vet even said that he is such a sweetheart.

When he first came home to us, he would go into the shed where my son practiced his guitar. During those same first days with us, I became sick. He would stay next to me in bed when he was finished keeping my son company in the shed. After we had him for about a week, he disappeared, and I panicked. He was locked in the shed, and when I found him there, I cried with relief.

My husband named him Ray. Ray got along nicely with the others, but Bart would bully and chase him every now and then. Sometimes, poor Ray reminded me of a loner. Occasionally, I think of an incident between him and Bart over feeding time. I have one large feeder for them all. They all know where to line up and take turns. This usually works very well for them. The feeder sits between an end table and couch. It is situated on the floor in a way that the dogs cannot eat from it. This is the only area in the whole house where it can be protected from the dogs' appetites. Once, when Bart insisted on going first to eat, he took so long that Ray did not want to wait any longer. Our passive Ray had a subtle plan. It was so cute how all you could see was one of Ray's oversized, toy-like paws sticking out from under the skirt of the couch. He was scooping up pebbles of food, falling out of the feeder as Bart ate. Ray was pulling them under the couch for himself. His paw disappeared under the skirt of the couch as he ate

RAY

them. You would not have known he was under there at all, but as he ate, the noisy crunches coming from under the couch gave him away. When Bart was finally done, Ray took his position at the feeder, and he ate until he also got his fill.

He is our little clown. He has done such antics as falling out of the ceiling tiles or swatting at us and the other animals from under the skirts of our chairs and couch. One time, however, this little clown made me cry by breaking some of my most treasured china with some of his unexpected acrobatics. I am pleased to say that I was able to salvage the china with some glue.

Every now and then Ray would disappear, and he would not come home until the next night around 10:00 p.m. He would do this like clockwork. Sometimes, I thought he had another home. Around this time in my life, I found out I had breast cancer and was going through treatments. I was sick and lost track of Ray. He was due home, but I thought it was not until the next night. I was wrong. He was due in that night, but he never made it home. The next morning our dear Ray, Ray, Raymond, Ray was found expired in the corner of our yard where he once romped and played.

It was Monday, May 23, 1994, 8:00 a.m., when my husband found him. He must have been on his way home, and he ran into trouble. Another animal followed and attacked him. Our dear Ray came to the end of his nine lives.

Ray, Ray, Raymond, Ray will live in our hearts forever just as Jessie girl does. When I now look at the glued broken china our little clown broke, I think of him and his lovable antics. As I start to smile, I am saddened with tears because I know he is not here to break more.

If it were up to me, none of our felines would ever go outside. I always breathe easier when they return to the house. Sometimes, when I walk by them outside in the yard, they will let me pick them up to carry them back into the house. I also will try coaxing them in with canned cat food. I will call them each by their name as I also call out, "Huff and Puff." This was the name of a canned cat food I used to feed them. They remember the name and come running. Sometimes, all I have to do is look at them and say, "Huff and Puff." They will respond immediately.

RAY

After they come inside and eat their treats, they usually run right back out like Australian boomerangs. The fastest boomerang is Bart because he is the hardest of all to keep in. I have to wait most of the time until they are ready to come in for a change either from the outdoors or in defeat of a hunt. Once they do settle in, you will always find them in their favorite spots. My little friends will be stationed throughout the house in sleeping poses. I will find them on the beds; seats of chairs; special rugs and windowsills; top of the couch or cabinets; etc. One of Ray's special places was the bathroom. Unless there was someone lying down with whom he could cuddle, you would usually find him on top of the little white cabinet above the commode. We nicknamed him "The Keeper of the Bathroom."

In my humble and sometimes futile attempts to protect them all in any way I can, I also put on each of them a safety collar with ID. Bart and Shinobi will remove theirs. Continually, I put these collars back on them, and they continually scratch them off or roll around on the ground until they come off. I am sure there are a couple of their collars still stuck in the top of our trees.

I had just as much of a hard time trying to keep a collar on Ray. I sometimes thought Ray had another home, and that was another reason why I tried to keep a collar on him. If he did have another home, it would let them know that Ray already had a loving family, and he was not a stray in need of a home. We all were extremely sad and upset to find Ray that morning in the corner of our yard. He was finally wearing his little yellow collar, which not only matched his creamy fur but also those large yellow eyes that will never open again.

What happened to Ray was sad beyond words. In the last chapter, I explain how this tragedy moved me forward with the awareness of what I have to do, as their owner, to protect them and the wildlife around us.

RAY

RAY

TEDDY

TEDDY

My mother told me as a child, when you are grieving over a lost pet, you must stop and go on to take care of the ones who still are alive and depending on you. Indeed, I do go on and on. We have added two more cats to our animal family, and they are Teddy and Abbey. Abbey is also known as "Shop Cat."

Teddy was found on a Tuesday, October 12, 1993. Actually, this was about five months before we lost Jessie and about seven months before losing Ray. He was a year old and weighed 9.4 lbs. My sons found him down the street from their father's office. They had to go to the store and walked by him, crying in a cardboard box, which was between a pair of marble steps. When they looked closer, they discovered he had a gash on his head over his left eye. His hair was matted; he looked weak and was scared to death. While still in his box, my two dear sons took him to the office. He would not move out of the box. There was an old gray pair of pants in there with him, and the box had a library number on it. I wish I had remembered the number because I would have played the lottery with it. Anyway, I do not know who left him in such a condition. Either he was abandoned this way or someone attempted to help him by giving him the box and old gray pair of pants for a soft bed. I can remember how heavily he purred as I petted him. This is something he still does.

In spite of his bushy tail, white paws and neck, along with the white around his nose and mouth, he still reminded me of Ray. Teddy's eyes are the same as Ray's eyes were, large and yellow but not quite as almond-shaped as his were. At the time, it was his basic coloring of creamy beige and sweet personality that really made me think of Ray.

First, I wanted to see if my mother could take him, but he would not get out of the box. We put his food and water in there with him, and this is how I had to put him into the car for our ride to see my mother.

I took him into my mother's home, box and all. In fact, he stayed in the box when I stopped for gas on the way to my mother's house. It was his home and his security. My mother was unable to take him. I knew this sweet and beautifully colored cat with such an outstanding bushy tail would never be without a loving home. I was right . . . my home!

TEDDY

Once he was in my home and found the surroundings agreeable with him, he finally came out of his box. He had to investigate all of our other animals. Maybe I should have called him Jack for "Jack in the Box?"

The sore on his head healed with no complications. Teddy is even more beautiful now since his hair has grown long and furry. His tail is gorgeous; it is twice as big and fluffy than when we first found him. His coat is clean and soft; it looks and feels like cotton. He also has been fattened up to weigh thirteen pounds. I think he is a Maine Coon. He looks like a little lion with long white hair hanging around his neck. His nose has a wide bridge and is covered with white fur, which makes his nose look even wider, enhancing his lion-like looks. It is neat how this white fur is in the shape of a triangle and encompasses his mouth.

Finding him was the same as finding a grab bag. I really did not know what I was getting at the time. Since we found him, he has gone through such a metamorphosis. Now, he is more than I ever expected in both appearance and personality. My mother often remarks how loving care has brought the beauty out in him and how she is sorry she could not have found a way to keep him. All I can say is, "It's too late, mom." "He's mine now."

When we first found him, I thought we had another Ray because he looked so passive and sweet in that box. I named him Teddy for Teddy Bear because I thought it was appropriate for this cuddly cat. I was wrong! While love and care brought the beauty out in his body, his personality blossomed into a "brat cat." He is, however, a lovable "brat cat," so the name Teddy still fits him. Even though he has done some real stunts around here, I still cannot call him a clown as I did Ray. Ted's actions are more diabolical. Lately, when we spot him, we say, "Here comes trouble!"

If he does not get what he wants or if you scold him, he will grab at your legs while running through the house and flipping through the air with such speed. Sometimes, we think he is flying. You can see the air blowing the long white fur around his neck along with the hair around his ears and paws. With all this hair going in every direction, it gives him the look of a wild man.

TEDDY

He will even take his frustrations out on the other cats and dogs by swatting at them. He is very highly spirited. Teddy has also jumped so high that he has hit the light switch and turned our lights on and off. Although this may seem innocent enough, if he knew what he was actually doing, he would do it over and over again to aggravate, irritate, and provoke! The one thing that will soothe him is to talk to him sweetly. He cannot handle it. They all love sweet talk but not as much as Teddy does. He just melts. Either sweet talk or a can of cat food will have a calming effect on Teddy.

Just the other night, he was pouting throughout the house, going from room to room. First, he would walk by; next, you would see him flying pass. Whenever your eyes met his, he meowed and took a swing at you. We knew he wanted more canned cat food. We were trying to cut him back because, if you would let him, he would eat a can every hour on the hour. When he saw Shinobi coming out of my youngest son's room, it was really the last straw for him. He jumped on her and gave her a smack. Poor Shinobi did not know what happened! She took cover in a secluded corner. He felt ignored because she was monopolizing my son's time, which in turn was keeping him from bringing out the canned cat food. Finally, we gave him more of what he wanted, and it wasn't sweet talk. He then settled down for the night and gave us some peace for that evening.

His love for canned cat food brings to mind another story: When we lost our Ray, we set a trap to make sure there was nothing living on our property that would be harmful to our pets. We put a can of cat food in the trap. The trap would let an animal in and hold him there unharmed until released. When the animals ran out of the house the next morning, we caught Ted in the trap. After all, what did we really think we were going to catch with a can of cat food for bait? Actually, Ted looked embarrassed to find himself stuck in the trap.

TEDDY

　　　Lately, I realize when you call, "Teddy," he is starting to respond as a dog would. He will come right to you no matter where he is. He is looking, of course, for a treat.
　　　It was because of Ted, I had to glue on every bud of my silk flower arrangement, which sits on our coffee table. Every morning, all the buds would be off, and I knew who picked them. I found them either on the floor or under the rugs and furniture. I then noticed how he started to wait until I went out before he would mutilate this flower. He did this knowing that upon my return, he would get a reaction from me.
　　　Ted does to Bart what Bart did to Ray. At times, he will run him, but he just wants to play. Bart will usually just take off because he is not familiar with being chased; he is usually the one doing the chasing. Occasionally, I do have to break up a scuffle between them.
　　　Ted and Ray, on the other hand, loved each other. Ted stayed in the house for six months before the different smells and sounds of nature allured him to the outdoors. Until that time, he would stay home patiently waiting for Ray to come back to play with him. When Ray came in, Ted would grab him around the neck, and Ray would grab Ted around his neck; they then playfully proceeded to pull each other to the floor. This rapport compensated for Bart's occasional raucous treatment of Ray. Ray did not seem like such a loner anymore because he had Ted for a wrestling partner.
　　　I also remember a Christmas with Ted and Ray. It was Ray's final Christmas. They wrestled with each other over the opened-boxes from our Christmas gifts. The less tired of the two was the winner and the one to sleep in the fought-over box. I understand why an emptied box would be such a treasure to Teddy as I recall how much he loved the box he was found in by my sons.
　　　After Ray died, Teddy really missed him. His little playmate was gone. The other cats were too fearful to take Ray's place because of Ted's rambunctious behavior.

TEDDY

Teddy does have a sparring partner now. It is Abbey. Ted's liveliness does not scare her, and she stands up to him. Abbey does not enjoy these encounters or surprise attacks from Ted as Ray did. She more or less tolerates them, and this interaction in itself is satisfying enough for her.

Ted does many other mentionable things, and he does one or two unmentionables! He sleeps with ceramic and stuffed animals as assimilations for either his mother or siblings.

When he now wants to get back into the house, he stands on the glider on the porch and scratches at the window until he gets our attention. If it is at night, all you can see is a big pink nose surrounded by white fur.

He has fallen into our hot tub. It was not covered only because I was in it at the time. When he jumped out with all that wet hair, he made our deck look as if he had swabbed it.

He also sticks out the tip of his tongue until we notice it. I also love the way he cups his big white paw to get the last morsel of food out of his bowl. He will grab at your arm with his nails and pull you back by your sleeve as he sits on his favorite windowsill, which is located in the bathroom. All you can see is a playful paw coming at you from between the closed curtain.

One day he sat on his favorite sill, struggling with the very last remains of his dinner in a can. I felt a tug on my sleeve as I walked pass his sill. I must have been distracted because I always make sure to put their food in bowls. As hard as he tried, he could not finish his food from this can. I then dumped it into his bowl as I usually do. There is no doubt in my mind that this time his tug on my sleeve was his way of getting my attention for help. That was all he wanted as he contentedly resumed eating.

Teddy now has us conditioned not to walk closely to that window for fear of being grabbed by the mysterious paw from behind the closed curtain.

TEDDY

    Ted also likes to hide under tablecloths. They drape over his face showing only his large pink nose, white whiskers, and his big white front paws. This sight will have you thinking you just saw a rabbit, and you should start looking for the Easter baskets.
    My husband even has an amusing tale to share with me about Teddy. We live on the water. One day when my husband went swimming, he looked up and saw Teddy spying on him from the end of our pier. He was holding onto the side of the pier with his large white paws, stretching his head over the water as far as his body would allow, enabling his wide yellow eyes to follow my husband as he swam back and forth.
    Out of all the cats, Teddy is the only one I will find inside the ferret's cage. He will use the ferret's litter pan or eat his food. Our poor ferret, Farrah Jo, is very confused and feels a bit displaced when Ted does this.
    Ted has another idiosyncrasy. For some strange reason the left side of his nose is always dirty. Every time I see him, I have to clean it. He simply "can't keep his nose clean."
    Ted's personality has incited the emotions of us all, cats, dogs, and ferret. This hairy live wire will either bring out the best in you or the worst.

TEDDY

ABBEY

ABBEY

Last is Abbey. She is also known as "Shop Cat." My oldest son found her in January 1995, during the day, in front of a vacant house. Knowing how cold it was going to be that night and how petite she was, he brought her into his father's office and named her "Shop Cat." She is black with a white chest, white stomach, and tiny white paws. She lived in the office where she loved everyone, and everyone loved her. She slept on desks' tops and was so happy to find shelter, food, and company. Someone always checked her on weekends. She seemed very content until she stopped eating. We noticed she spent too much time curled up sleeping. Everyone knew something was wrong. We took her to our vet, and he explained how she developed a blood disorder from previous insect bites. She received these bites from living on the streets. "Shop Cat" stayed at the animal hospital for over a week before she was able to return to the office. When back in the office, she was her old self again, eating better than ever.

"Shop Cat" is a name everyone at the animal hospital loved and recognized. When I called to check on her, right away they would say, "Shop Cat" is doing fine." "She is eating like a horse and gaining the weight she needs." In addition, I am told that she is anywhere from two to four years old. This is hard to believe because of her petite size. Her age makes me wonder if she ever was a mother and what kind she would have been? I can imagine her being a protective, dedicated mom as she took care of her kittens with tender, loving care yet daring anyone or anything to harm them. When we found her, she was not spayed and most likely lived on the streets all of her life. It is hard to believe that she never had kittens.

Next, we took her to be spayed. Upon doing so, the doctor informs us she has a tumor on her uterus. Later, we are relieved to learn it is benign.

When we brought "Shop Cat" back to the office after her operation, we felt she might be getting too lonesome there by herself at night. Even our trips to the office on Saturdays and Sundays to check on her, did not seem to break her boredom. On those more recent trips to check her, we also had to give her the rest of the medicine she needed for her previous illness. She took her pills like such a good little girl.

ABBEY

"Shop Cat" would look so lonesome in the window or in her chair where she would lie on an old sweater, listening to the TV. This is how we would find her in the mornings. To keep her company, we always left on the TV. When we would leave, we had to sneak out so she could not follow us.

Because there were so many animals at home, we tried to keep her in the office. I just could not stand it any longer to think of how lonesome she must be in the office all by herself. That night, I went to visit her with my youngest son. There she was, curled up on the chair, as usual, with her old sweater and looking so forlorn. She was extremely happy to see us. She meowed and started rubbing her head on us. I brought "Shop Cat" home that night.

She interacted with the other cats and dogs with skepticism. When she walked pass the dogs, she would hiss and give them a smack with her little white paw. The dogs just watched her with bewilderment and knew better than to retaliate.

"Shop Cat" soon learns that all are welcome here with plenty of food and water. She also finds out the hard way that nothing less than a reasonable aura of tranquility is expected from her, especially when it comes to Shinobi.

"Shop Cat" would give our Shinobi a fit. She would stalk and chase her. I could only keep Shinobi in the house just long enough for her to eat before running out again. Once outside, you could not find her anywhere until she was ready to come back in to eat. She probably was upset thinking she had lost her home to the new arrival. I was afraid I would lose Shinobi. If she stayed out too long, she might wander off looking for a new home. I also did not want a repeat of what happened to our Ray. Shinobi has such a timid personality, and I really worried about the negative chemicals between these two females. Whatever was going on between them, seemed to upset Shinobi worse than any confrontations she had in the past with Jessie. I really had to work on this problem. I took a spray bottle of water and sprayed "Shop Cat" every time she started to stalk Shinobi. I made sure, of course, not to aim at her face or ears. By using this technique, she learned to leave Shinobi alone, and her adverse behavior was not allowed in our home. They now get along together just fine.

ABBEY

The next thing I had to do was to change her name, "Shop Cat." Even though the staff at the animal hospital preferred to call her "Shop Cat," I found it too awkward to call her that. There were times, however, I did find myself wanting to call her "Fat Lady in the Circus" because of how heavy she was getting. This, of course, was not a fit name either for our new cat, but I do think it is cute to call her it every now and then. She had another name or handle in her personality that was worth finding. She needed a new name, not only to suit her better, but it had to slide off your tongue more readily as you called for her. It took awhile, but my youngest son and I agreed on what we believed to be a fair and decent name for her. She is finally starting to answer to her new name as we call out, "Abbey, Abbey, Abbey."

Now that she is so fat, when she stands up on her hind legs to reach for something, her big white stomach reminds me of a potbellied stove with little thin legs, and her little black nose looks like a tiny chunk of coal. Her body has outgrown her petite head, legs, and paws. This was the opposite of Jessie whose body had to catch up with her head.

At the present, I am happy to say that I am keeping Abbey in the house, and she is listening to me. I hope it stays this way, especially with all of her past medical problems. She did get outside once. Inadvertently, the screen was up on one of our first floor windows. When I noticed it, I also realized I had not seen Abbey for a while. I ran outside calling her. Instantly, I heard her meow back as she desperately ran towards me, to tell me of her horrible experience. Abbey thought she was lost because she did not know how to get back in through the window. It was obviously easier for her to jump down from this window than to jump back up into it. After I grabbed and hugged her, I petted her all the way back to the safety of the indoors. When I returned with her, I immediately gave her a treat to settle her down. Abbey seemed relieved to be home and contented to stay there, which was unlike the others who cannot wait to run out again.

Whenever I give out treats, she is always there. She will come moseying over to get a piece of the action along with whatever other cats are in the house at the time.

ABBEY

Abbey deserves every treat she gets because she is a sweet girl to stay in on such a permanent basis.

Abbey reminds me often of Jessie, and I unconsciously call her Jessie. If she is surprised by a certain touch or petted unexpectedly, she will respond as Jessie did by purring, "Hmmmmm?" In addition, she can take up for herself just as Jessie was able to do for herself. They both had their share of medical problems from trying to survive on the streets. Abbey, however, other than being overweight, is now a much healthier cat than when we found her. I am so relieved that I was able to save Abbey from the streets. I was able to do for her what I ultimately was unable to accomplish for our dear, late Jessie.

Abbey also reminds me of my Jessie girl when she comes into the bathroom while I am bathing in the tub. She jumps up on the tub and tiptoes around the side of it. Jessie did it to be nosy and enjoyed listening to the splashing of water, whereas Abbey does it to corner me into rubbing her head. She never gets enough rubbing on the sides of her face. She will push her face into anything: plants, furniture, or your face. She will meow at you as she looks for a free hand by which to be touched. She will not let you stop before you find yourself vigorously massaging the sides of her head. At times, Abbey has even used her small paw to lift my hand so she could put her head under it to be rubbed. When you are sleeping, she will lie on top of you waiting and looking for a moving hand under which to place her head. She also lies above you in bed, watching over you. Actually, she is most likely looking for any sign that you will give her a few more minutes of rubbing.

On several occasions, I have found Abbey kneading on stuffed animals while she nestled her head into their soft bodies. When she does this, she is having a flashback of being a kitten and nursing.

She is also the only one of my cats who will scratch and dig in their litter box until it starts shaking and moving around as though a fifty-pound dog were in it.

I am very pleased to say that Abbey is still getting along well with Shinobi. They are starting to touch noses as Shinobi does with Bart. Abbey will box with Teddy using both front paws. We

ABBEY

call it "double pawing." Bart and Abbey do their best to ignore each other, but if there is any hostility, it will be on Abbey's part. Bart will then simply find his own corner. He does not want anything to do with her.

The most adorable thing about Abbey is her loyalty. She is always by your side. She is very dear and personable. Now that she knows her name, she will come when you call her. You can always depend on her to be there to cuddle with you whether it is on the couch, in bed, or next to you in a chair. Most of the time, I wake up with her sleeping on top of me, and I find myself saying, "You'll have to move Fat Lady." Our Abbey is always close by for rubs and love. Even now, as I write, she is behind me curled up on the floor and waiting for me to finish for the night. Actually, they will all come and spend time with me as I work at my desk.

When the others want to join Abbey and me, they will either sit on the desk or stand in an opened-desk drawer as I type. They use the drawer as an observation deck to see me better and get a closer look at what I am doing. There are times that I have to stop writing to get one of them to move off the paper. There are also times when I have to get up from the desk to let one of them in from the balcony. They hear me typing and come to the balcony door. They will scratch at its screen until I let them in. Once they are in, they beat me to my seat, and I have to scoot them to move. It reminds me of playing musical chairs.

Abbey is always, however, the one to be there and to wait the longest for me. She will then follow me downstairs where I will repay her for her company with a small bowl of skim milk. On one of those nights, she fell asleep so soundly waiting for me that she did not know I was finished working and ready to go downstairs. When I picked her up, she awoke asking me what I wanted as she purred, "Hmmmmm?" After I carried her to the kitchen for a little treat of skim milk, I looked at her and lovingly said, "Mommy's Fat Baby."

ABBEY

ABBEY

FAMILY PHOTOS

"TOBIE"

OUR NEWEST BABY

FARRAH JO

ZENEY

CHUCKIE

MIDNIGHT

ALVIN

MOLLY

HELP
also known as
HELPIE

ALVIN

MANDY

PRECIOUS

A LOVING GLANCE

A LOVING GLANCE

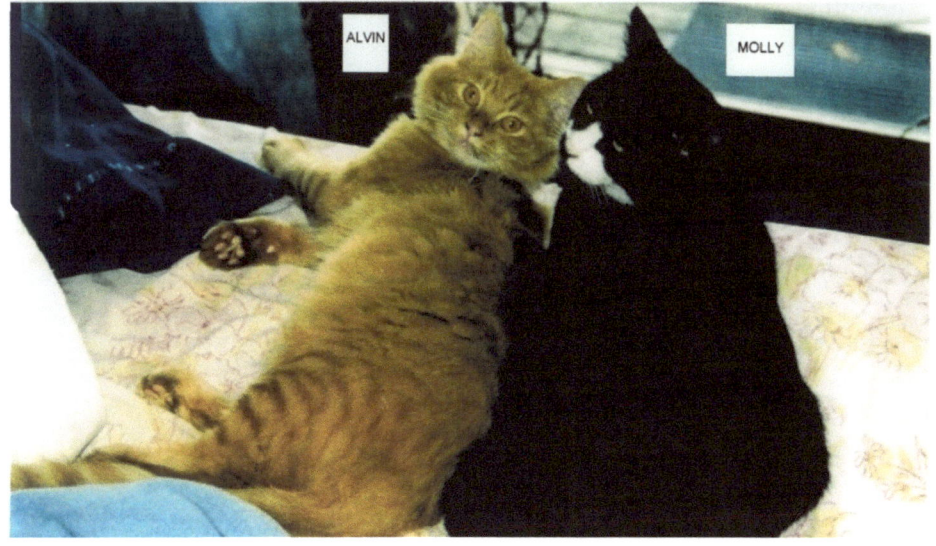

A LOVING GLANCE

When I rescued my more recent dog, Benny, I had so many pets that he thought his name was "Wait-a-minute." For the most part, we all get along with only minor indifferences. Our female dog, Ginger, will give a little growl at one of the felines if she thinks they are getting too close to one of her chew bones. She might also give a little growl out of jealousy if one of them tries to move in on her time with us humans. While giving Bart and Shinobi treats, Bart will finish his first and then check on Shinobi to see if she has any left. He will then give her a little nudge in hopes of also getting the rest of her treat. If nudging does not work, he will give her a light smack with his paw. I have to step in to keep things fair because Shinobi is so submissive. Occasionally, there are scuffles I have to break up between the two males, Ted and Bart. Other than some small infractions as these, there is blessed congeniality. They all will curl up and sleep together in our beds. They will also eat their treats together and usually without a problem, and they have learned to take turns at the feeder. It is safe to say that we are one big, happy family.

There are times that I think of them all as little gremlins, going about their business in my home. Sometimes, they will not even acknowledge me. They have all brought a mixture of personalities into our household. We have had a sweetheart of a clown, Ray; a rough, tough cowgirl, Jessie; the gentle prima donna, Shinobi; my half angel and half devil doorman, Bart; our lovable brat, Teddy; and, of course, our dear, loyal fat lady, Abbey.

Their lives are so much better now than when we found them that I think of them all as winning the lottery. They have at their disposal furniture, beds, and sills upon which to sleep. There is plenty of food for all and treats for just staying within the safe confines of our house. When they run out, they have a large yard with trees to play and exercise as they pass the time of day. I try to keep them safer by not giving them their treats during the day so they will still be looking for them later. I am then better able to coax them inside before dark with the treats. They will be safer, of course, not roaming at night.

They have medical care. I have taken them to the vet even on days I did not feel well. On one of those visits, I found myself telling the vet my symptoms. He said, "Get plenty of rest and fluids." I thankfully said, "I am so glad I got to talk to a doctor!"

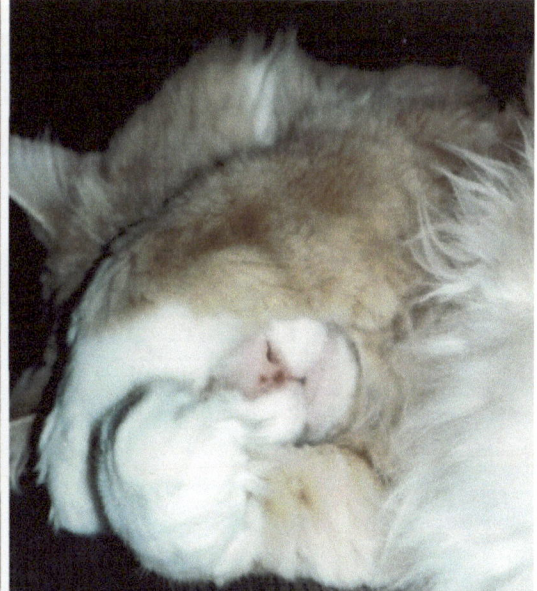

A LOVING GLANCE

Then we laughed as I told him how my animals just received better medical care than I did because I was unable to get an appointment with my doctor for the day.

Yes, they are all winners but so are we, for each one of them is an indispensable addition to our family. I have learned so much through them, and I enjoy them every day in so many different ways. I find comfort in watching them sleep. They will be sprawled by the woodstove in such cute poses with their paws over their eyes or under their chins. I enjoy watching how cozy they are lying on top of furniture with their front paws tucked so neatly under their furry chests. When they do this with their paws, they remind me of little old, sleepy men and women trying to keep warm on a cold, snow-filled day by sticking their hands up the sleeves of their oversized-sweaters.

As they sleep, they look so tired from eating and playing all day. I have to laugh when I see them sleeping on the bed; they are so stretched out that they look as if they were spilt.

I also enjoy watching as they clean themselves with such precision. While lying in bed with me one morning, Bart cleaned his head so much by rubbing it with his well-licked paw that he gave himself a new hairdo. His hair stood straight up on his head. While Bart was waiting for me to wake up, he was so bored and did not know what else to do.

They purr me to sleep every night with their little humming motors. I am overwhelmed some mornings by their thoughtfulness; they would have left outside the front door what they believed to be a breakfast plate for my family and me. It will usually be a fat dead mouse and even a mole at times.

I love to watch them knead at the blankets as if they were kneading dough. This movement is a residual from their baby days, massaging their mothers for milk.

It is amusing how they all have such large yawns. They remind me of lions in a circus with mouths so wide that the trainer can stick his head into them.

It tickles me and gives me such pleasure to have my feline companions communicate with me in any way they can. It could

A LOVING GLANCE

be Bart tapping at my hand to open the door for him; Teddy pulling at my arm to help him with his food; Shinobi singing to disclose to us her needs and desires; or Abbey's sweet and short meows as she pleads for attention and to be rubbed.

They all have their own meows. When Bart is really feeling mellow, he will just move his mouth to meow, but nothing comes out. This contributes to his look of serenity. Ted has straight forward cries to get what he wants. Ray had a deep meow, which sounded stuck in his throat. Jessie's sounded as if someone had been plucking at their guitar.

Each will vocalize and communicate in their particular way, but they all have eyes that reveal an illumination in which you could drown. Perhaps what I am really seeing in those illuminating eyes is the unique enlightenment that each feline holds through his mystical sixth sense.

When interacting with them, I am on the threshold of two worlds. In one of these, I understand their basic needs. While the other holding the secrets of all animals, is a world to which no comparisons can be made. What human arrogance it is to compare their intellect to ours or their motivations to be moralized! I have brought them into my world and in the most endearing way, share this with you. In my humble attempt to lovingly capture the personalities of these mystic creatures, I am also on some level guilty of this arrogance, but after all, I am only human.

Because of them, I have plenty of loose hair to be vacuumed, holes in my screens, tears in my furniture, scratches on my molding, and glued knickknacks on my shelves. They even use my lawn furniture more than I do. I know they were there first because of their hair left behind. They are now such a big part of my life that I cannot remember it being any other way.

There is always room for one more. Every new personality brought amongst us, however, changes the interactions of all. I am taking a chance each time there is an adoption of a new family member. I do not know what bad habits he or she might have and how it will consequently change the way they all will interact. Once the harmony is broken, I also do not know what it will take to bring it back again or how long it will take. This is the chance I am now always willing to take since I have realized the personal growth and fulfillment I have received in return from my encounters with every one of them.

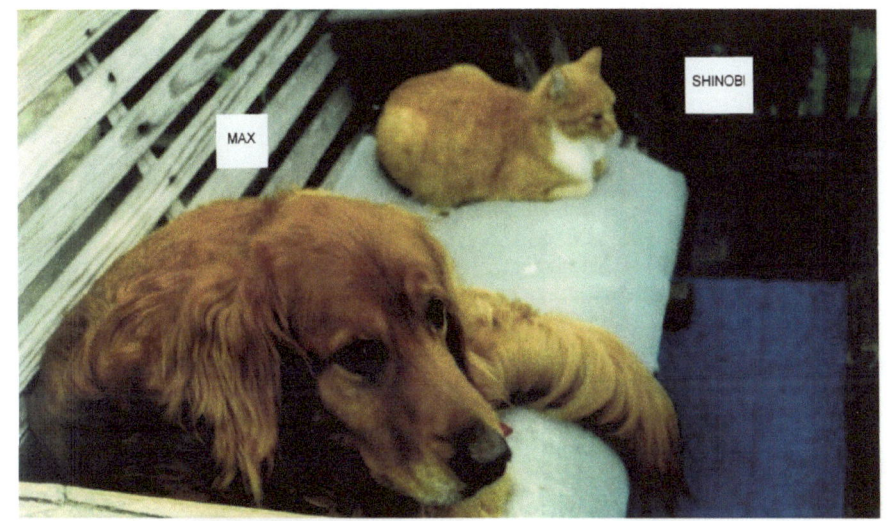

A LOVING GLANCE

    Their greatest and most personal gift to me is that they are what they are. They have no agendas or ulterior motives. They are true to themselves, their species, and the animal kingdom. There will never be any deviation from that. This is something we can depend on and trust to the end. I have been accepted into their world. With this connection, I feel whole; I am being balanced on the border of two worlds through which I have learned acceptance, tolerance, and love for all of God's creatures.

    All of this is mine for the price of a can of cat food!

A BETTER WAY

A BETTER WAY

Since the writing of this book, I have learned a lot but mostly, to take more control. Our felines simply do not go out anymore. I found that I could deter them from running outside by spraying them with a spray bottle of clean water, which I also did to Abbey to keep her from stalking Shinobi. I also discovered by filling a small empty coffee can with pennies and shaking it at them will scare them away from the door. These techniques have successfully worked. They have finally gotten the message that I do not want them outside. There is too much danger outside for them and too much that they can harm. Just by keeping a feline from consuming the wildlife, takes away the worry of him getting toxoplasmosis, of course, unless he has already been infected, or he is eating raw and undercooked meats. There is also less chance of a cat getting tapeworms from ingesting an infected flea. By keeping my cats in, I will be protecting them all in so many ways and stopping their destruction of wildlife.

The most significant change was my mentality over the control issue. I felt uneasy taking control in this way. It always was hard for me to say no to them. I was now taking away their freedom. A part of me connected with their love of freedom. Maybe I found a sense of release for my own emotional congestion while watching and enjoying them as they did what was natural for them. It was much more than this. I now realize the salvaging of these little creatures as they lovingly came into my life, put me through a deep emotional housecleaning. They set me free. They gave me hope and inspiration! When I could no longer keep them in, I ultimately accepted it as what they had to do. When they would return safely, it was positive reinforcement of all I found to be right with the way we interacted. It was a full circle of reciprocation. In this, I found a sense of stability and continuity. I now understand that as they traveled in and out, I perceived it as a part of the same inspired freedom they helped me find. I now had to take it away from them and break the circle.

Reality hit home with the loss of Ray. When Ray died that morning, so did a part of my inspired heart. They do not travel outside any longer. I feel I am now a more responsible owner with this decision. Losing Ray and seeing the destruction of wildlife they can cause, initiated this change. Once I discovered the spray bottle of water and can of pennies were good techniques, I knew I could and should change things. This change is bearable because I know it is right for me to protect them and the wildlife surrounding us.

A BETTER WAY

It is still very important to keep safety collars on them with their IDs in case they do get out. Their IDs have the needed information to help return them if they get lost. If their names are on the IDs, they can be lured away. I no longer put a bell on any cat collar because a bell can become caught on something, their claws can also become caught in it, and they can swallow it. Another reason is that their ears are sensitive, and the sound of a bell is louder to them than it is to a person. Safety collars will either stretch or break away from around their necks before they can hang themselves on anything. This is very important for them because of how active they are and why regular collars are not recommended. Do not put a collar on a kitten. You should research what age is safe to do so. Do not make cats' collars too snug or too loose. The space of two flat fingers between their collars and necks can be used as a guideline. If this is a stretch collar, do not stretch it to accomplish this because it will make it too tight. Use your judgment to test the fit: not so loose that it can become caught on something or he is able to get his leg or jaw dangerously caught in it, which he can also do while eating, drinking, or grooming. A collar caught under his arm can become embedded. A cat can become twisted in the elastic and strangle before he can get out of it, but do not make it too snug that it is uncomfortable or harmful. Make sure the stretch collar will stretch enough so he can escape if needed, but not so much elastic that he can become twisted in it. Recheck the fit because while putting it on him, he might have tensed his neck muscles and if so, readjust it. Putting it on with his chin up as he stands or sits, might help. Make sure an adjustable safety collar cannot slip so the adjustments you made to give it a proper fit will not change, especially if he or another pet is pulling on it. Watch so neither pet becomes entangled. As your pet grows and an elastic collar gets old, don't consider the old, relaxed elastic in it as a good fit; he needs a new collar with new elastic and fitted properly again. It might have dangerously stretched just enough for his jaw or leg to become caught in it.

An actual quick release collar is not a break-away collar. A break-away collar will come apart on its own if your pet becomes entangled or even if another pet's mouth is also caught in the collar and needs to escape. The problem I am hearing is that some of these collars are not breaking away. Make sure it is truly a break-away collar and not one you need to release. You need to make sure it breaks away under pressure and leverage is not an issue for it to release! Check out the different plastic prongs and research which are the better break-away ones. It will not have a locked position. They are bought by size and cat's weight so under pressure, if your cat is entangled on something or with another cat, whose mouth might have become caught in the collar while playing, it will release on its own to set them free. Try hanging weight off it. The weight should only be the same weight as your cat, to see if it will break away properly for him and without needing leverage. In addition, test the break-away collar to make sure it is not too hard to pull apart even when twisted, and also leverage is not needed for it to easily break away to release him.

Another issue with the cat break-away collars is that some will break away too easily. Hopefully, you will find the right one for your cat. You can also find them on websites.

Either make sure the elastic collar or break-away collar you use works correctly and your cat is use to his before you stop keeping a close eye on him. Get him use to just the collar, and then try it with the ID added. This could take a few days of you putting it on and taking it off him so he wears it only while you can closely watch him. It is so important for either kind of these collars to have the correct fit, keeping in mind two flat fingers as a guideline. The elastic collar: comfortable while he is still able to escape from it without it twisting from too much slack; his jaw or leg cannot dangerously become stuck in it; and the collar unable to become caught on anything. The break-away collar should be TESTED and fitted properly so it is unable to become caught while it is still comfortable on him. There are so many variations of the elastic safety collars to research; you should be able to find the right one that works as you expect by testing its fit. Become familiar with some of the sad stories when it is not fitted properly. Fitting an elastic safety collar correctly can be a bit tricky. Unless you are familiar with the use of the elastic safety collars and your cat is doing fine with one, I suggest a tested and proven to be a true break-away collar to someone looking into cat safety collars. You should always have an extra collar with ID in case he loses his.

There are also important things to remember about our canine friends. If their names are on their IDs, they can be lured away. The guideline of two flat fingers also applies to fitting dog collars; maybe use three fingers for a large dog such as a Great Dane. Their collars should be able to spin around their necks with just some friction. If there is more friction, they could be too snug. If they spin freely, they could be too loose. They should be both comfortable and safe for them. Use your judgment. They should not be too snug, but if they are too loose, they will be able to back out of the collars and run away while being walked on a leash. In addition, they could dangerously become caught on something.

 Look also into the break-away collars for them. If they become entangled or if IDs, licenses, or any necessary medical tags on them are dangerously caught, they will break away. This probably would also be good for active puppies. Check to make sure they work correctly and break away as they should. As with the feline break-away collars, make sure it is truly a break-away collar. Test the break-away collar to make sure it is not too hard to pull apart, and your dog's weight will cause it to break away to release him if caught, especially if you have a small breed dog. If you have a small breed dog, you could try a cat break-away collar for his ID. You would need a harness for his walks because a cat break-away collar will not have a safety override feature for walks on a leash and will break away if used while walking your dog. Make sure, however, the cat break-away collar is for the right weight of your dog, example: small 5 lb. dog and not for a 10 lb. cat! Take notice that some cat collars have settings for the pet's weight, but they still need to be checked and watched. A true break-away collar should release your pet or another pet whose mouth might have also become caught in the collar while playing. Make sure it will break away under the pressure of only your dog's weight, and leverage does not play a part in its release even when pulled or twisted, making sure it will break away easily enough to release your dog if caught. If you grab your pet by this collar, it will break away from his neck, unless the safety feature is overridden with a leash. Use the general guideline of two flat fingers to make sure it is comfortable with a proper fit so it cannot become caught on something, causing it to break away. Keep in mind an actual quick release collar is not a break-away collar. If your pet is so entangled or another pet's mouth is caught in his collar, and there is a dangerous struggle, you might not be able to get to the quick release for a rescue or even be there! If you can get to it, you might not have the needed slack to release it. Make sure the break-away collar you personally find to be safe for your dog will have a safety override feature for walks such as two metal rings. One ring is on each side of the snap so you can attach a leash to them, preventing it from breaking away while going for a walk. If fitted correctly, he will not be able to pull out of the collar.

 Watch that all pets' ID tags are durable and stay readable. If you over do it with tags, it might be uncomfortable for your pet.

A BETTER WAY

Hooks for tags can become caught, especially the ones that look like the figure eight. Look into non-hanging IDs that cannot become caught but make sure they are used only on collars you deem to be safe for your dog or cat. There is a slip-on collar ID tag, ID embroidery on the collar that can be easily seen, or an ID tag riveted onto the collar. Make sure the rivets are smooth, especially inside the collar.

 A choke chain should never be left on your dog as his regular collar. It can become caught on something, pull tight, and strangle him. This applies also to any collar or strap that can function in this way! A choke chain is only for training sessions or to help handle the dog. You must know the correct way to use one; it can do damage, and never use one on a puppy. I also heard they are no longer recommended. Look into more humane methods to achieve what is wanted. Also, make sure adjustable collars are the ones that once an adjustment is made, they cannot slip and accidentally tighten or loosen, especially if pulled on by the pets.

 Both cats and dogs should always wear correctly fitted collars. Always keep an eye on how their collars are fitting them, and they are still working as you expect. It is also important to do this as they grow, lose or gain weight, as their coats change, and because some collars will stretch or shrink. Recheck collars after pets are groomed because their collars would have been removed.

 Some dogs should only wear harnesses for walking because harnesses will not pull on their throats, causing damage or raising the pressure in their eyes. Small breed dogs, puppies, and active dogs might do better with harnesses. A short-snouted dog should wear a harness for his walks because it is easier for him to breathe without anything pulling on his throat. In addition, dogs with thick necks but have small heads would benefit from wearing harnesses because collars will slip right over their heads. Still, keep collars on all of them at all times that are safe and correctly fitted with IDs. When your dog wears a harness for walking, research to find the right one for him and learn how to fit it on him so he will not be able to slip out of it on his walks while also being comfortable. Take the harness off your dog after his walk. Finally, when pets are in cages or crates, remove all collars, etc. so they cannot become caught.

 A leash can also be the actual culprit in strangulation when it is attached to the dog's collar. What if a dog's leash is caught on a porch higher than his leash is long and he jumps, or he can fit through the rails, or a leash caught in an elevator door? Even the

A BETTER WAY

break-away collar can only help when the leash is unhooked to free the break-away safety feature so the collar can break away.

There are so many products on the market and information to research so you are better equipped to have for your pet the right collar/harness with the correct fit, keeping him both safe and comfortable. The different kinds of tags, reflective products for night, etc. should be checked to make sure all work the way expected and are safe for your pets to use. I need to mention that the retractable leashes are dangerous.

I like the safety break-away collars for all pets, especially cats, puppies, small dogs, and all active dogs as long as you have tested and proven them to be truly break-away collars, releasing under the right pressure and not depending on leverage even when pulled and twisted. These collars can break away if grabbed for a rescue, but they also can break away if grabbed to steal your pet.

Permanent identification of your pet is so important. It can increase your chances of finding him. An injected microchip can be a successful recovery method. Your vet can give you more information in reference to permanent identifications.

It is better to have a readily visible ID on your dog or cat than no collar at all even if your dog or cat has a microchip, and your cat is a house cat. If he gets lost without a readily visible ID on him, you are still taking a chance of not having him returned. Visible ID plays a big part in having your lost pet returned versus what mishaps can occur if not wearing one.

I explain different scenarios to try to bring to light some red flags for you to be aware of about your pet's collar. I encourage you when making a decision for your dog or cat, to do your own investigation by way of reading reliable materials and seeking the professional advice needed on this topic to confirm the correctness of these scenarios for both his safety and comfort. Hopefully, with this knowledge, common sense, and good judgment, you will find what is right for your pet.

Since they do not go out anymore, I have modified a room upstairs for them. Along with their usual run of the house, this helps to add to their everyday activities. In that room I have carpet-covered shelves where I find them comfortably snoozing. It is where they find most of their toys and a lamp with moving fish, which they love to watch. From that room, there is plenty to view of the outside through a large patio door. They also have a special box with a little blanket by the window in our living room. They take turns sleeping in it and looking out of the window from it.

A BETTER WAY

The windows are sturdy with full screens to keep our cats from falling out. This will keep them from injury or even death. Look into pet screening because of their ability to scratch open screens. Do some research to keep your pet safe in your windows.

I have learned that fish cat foods, dry and canned, can cause urinary tract infections, especially in the neutered males. It is best to buy foods having low ash and low magnesium to help prevent these urinary tract infections. Try the poultry canned cat foods. Actually, a diet of dry cat food is not healthy for your cat because of the high carbohydrates, low water content, and the plant-based proteins versus the animal-based proteins. When they do eat dry cat food, make sure they drink plenty of fresh water with it to prevent kidney damage. They have a low thirst drive and need plenty of water whenever they eat. I now feed mine canned cat food because it has animal-based proteins and contains more water, preventing kidney damage. Canned poultry is the best for their kidneys. If the canned food has by-products in it, I think it is still healthier for a cat's kidneys than the dry foods; however, I am not saying to feed them by-products. Patiently, ease into changing their diets. They should only eat small amounts of food high in vitamin A such as liver. Food with corn (maize), wheat, or soy is not healthy for your pets. Soy can also contribute to thyroid problems. Know the bad preservatives in your pets' foods and avoid them. Become knowledgeable of what is actually in their foods, what their needs are, and what they are actually eating.

Do not feed your cats a people-tuna diet. It can be fatal for them. Also, never keep food from them; it can be dangerous to their health. Instead, if they are overweight, correct this problem with more playtime activities and talk with your vet for help.

Before you buy the treats that can help to keep their teeth clean, make sure they are not the ones causing health issues.

Milk products are hard on a cat's digestive system and can cause diarrhea. Lactose intolerance can be a real problem. Plenty of fresh water is the best for your cat. There are a couple of interesting things about cats and their drinking water: some like running water, and some can detect chlorine in their water.

They should always have plenty of fresh water available to them in regularly cleaned bowls. Use a nonabrasive scrubber to clean them. Make sure you rinse all detergents well from their bowls. Look into ways to give them pure water free of contaminants. Do not let them drink from places such as the toilet or Christmas tree stand. High quality stainless steel would be the

A BETTER WAY

best kind of bowls for both their water and food. Ceramics might have a lead glaze, colors, or designs. Plastic can also be toxic and holds bacteria.

I safe proof my trash by smashing tin cans and plastic containers. I will thoroughly rinse out glass jars along with any other containers, etc. that will not smash well enough; then I tightly replace the also well-cleaned lids before putting them in the trash or recycling bin. All of this is done to avoid the hazards of an animal being able to get his head stuck in a can, jar, etc. or his tongue and mouth cut while looking for food.

When driving, do not make a stop and leave your pet in the car. A pet can expire in just slightly warm weather even if the windows are down enough for him to have a flow of air. All are in danger, especially the short-snouted ones. Remember all, long-snouted and short-snouted can expire in this way in a short time.

Another issue that makes me shudder is air travel and pets. He will be exposed to extreme temperatures. The cargo hold must be pressurized, temperature-controlled, and ventilated. If it is temperature-controlled, it will not be while the plane is on the tarmac even with delays. He will not be accessible to you, and you have no control over his care. Research what your pet will go through along with all the dos and don'ts. Your pet will be exposed to danger and trauma. He might not make it! If he cannot safely travel with you, can he stay with someone whom he likes and can be trusted to keep him safe and meet his needs? Boarding your pet until you get back can also be stressful for him.

If they are watching at the door, it makes me think they need to search for grass. Either their stomachs are bothering them or they are dealing with hair balls and want to eat grass to help them vomit. Grass acts as a laxative for them, which can also help with their hair balls. Too much will give them diarrhea. You can grow indoor grass for them, purchased at different pet stores, and it will be free of any toxic lawn chemicals. There are also products on the market for hair balls. If they keep eating grass to vomit, there might be a need to visit the vet. My one cat was always looking for grass. The vet told me he had a kidney disease, which was upsetting his stomach. He then received the appropriate care. I have heard that pets also eat grass to relieve joint aches and to help fight infections. Ask your vet which kind of grass will agree with your cat. Grass will irritate their stomachs, which helps them vomit, but if they do this too often, it can cause chronic gastritis.

I have had luck using catnip when introducing a new cat

A BETTER WAY

into the household. Make sure it is 100% certified organic catnip and has no long or hard pieces of stalk in it. They also seem to enjoy eating a small amount after vomiting or vomiting hair balls. I was told some cats become aggressive when catnip is given to them. Also, do not give catnip to aging cats, obese cats, cats with heart problems, or diabetic cats. When catnip is excessively ingested, it will cause vomiting and diarrhea. Actually, I have heard many interesting things about both grass and catnip. I suggest animal lovers draw their own conclusions by investigating these issues through the appropriate books or websites and, of course, talking it over with their vets.

Cats are also prone to heart problems. If they have coughs other than with their hair balls, I take them to the vet to have this checked. It could be a heart problem or another medical issue.

SNAP, which stands for Spay Neuter Assistance Program, can help with the price of spaying and neutering your pet, which is very important to have done. Check to see if your vet takes Snap Certificates. To keep my felines healthy, they also have their exams and vaccines to help protect them against diseases. Learn about the different side effects associated with some vaccines and the controversy with the over-vaccinating of your pet.

The vet told me the Leukemia shot is not recommended unless any one of them goes outside. Ask your vet about this. Feline Leukemia is an incurable disease and is infectious to other cats. If your cat has this disease, your vet can explain options other than euthanasia.

I will not declaw my cats. No vet could make me feel right about it. It involves amputating the last bone joint of each toe on the front paws. There are different methods, and all are mutilating. Once a cat is declawed, it affects his ability to grasp and climb. If he falls into something dangerous, he will not be able to remove himself from it. He should not be allowed to escape to the dangers of outside, especially now. He can develop behavioral problems, an abnormal stance, and even lameness. If he is unable to scratch to leave his scent, he might resort to other methods such as spraying. Also, there might be urinating issues. I would like to mention, a behavioral problem could be an actual medical issue and needs to be brought to the attention of your vet. If it is a behavioral issue, there are professionals who can help. One should research and understand all the permanent side effects a feline might encounter because he was declawed. To help with the claws, you should have different, sturdy scratching devices that will not

A BETTER WAY

fall over as he stretches his body and leans on them to scratch. Try rubbing some catnip on them to draw his attention. The actual scratching material should be made of materials he likes such as cardboard, jute, sisal, Berber, or untreated wood that will not splinter. If he scratched your furniture once, he will do it again until his scent is removed with a neutralizer that is both safe for him and your furniture. The vet can also clip his claws. It is best to have them clipped by someone who knows what they are doing unless you learn how. The pink part inside of the nail is called the quick, and it is sensitive even to pressure. If it is mistakenly cut, it will be painful and bleed. There are products to put on it to help with the pain and bleeding. To reiterate, please do not attempt clipping them unless you know how. There is a filing device for your pet's nails. You can look into the ways suggested to help your pet become accustom to the filing device. There are also caps to cover the claws.

    Reliable cat books and different websites can also offer a lot of helpful information. They can aid in your research of all the critical reasons not to declaw and give you great insight on feline behavior. This knowledge will open your mind to your pet's needs and help in finding alternatives to declawing such as techniques and products to help deter him from scratching, along with how to care for his claws. Read up on feline pheromones for behavioral issues.

    After becoming knowledgeable about this subject, I made a decision not to declaw. I hope all feline owners will come to this same conclusion.

    In addition, a reliable book on cats' basic health can make you aware of very important issues you need to know: You should never give your pet chocolate, grapes, or raisins; and the dangers of them ingesting antifreeze, chemicals, alcohol, cleaners, and medications. If these substances are in places where he will walk or sleep, it can also enter his system as he cleans and grooms himself. Be careful of houseplants; they can be poisonous for a cat. One should never medicate a pet on their own. He is sensitive and can easily have toxic reactions. For example, acetaminophen as found in Tylenol and other products, is deadly for your pet. Also, there is a clear plastic pilling syringe to help with his medicines. This book should be informative enough to make you aware of all medical issues your cat is prone to having along with the symptoms and preventions. Make sure it has a list of all the toxic plants, substances, and foods.

A BETTER WAY

These same sources will have information on effective, safe litters and pans for your cat and household. They also can help with recognizing unsafe toys for him and safe proofing your home: You don't want to find out the hard way the hazards of blind cords, plastic bags, reclining chairs, rocking chairs; or the dangers of hot stove tops, lit candles, electric wires; and the choking factor associated with strings, feathers, rubber bands, and small objects. There are also hidden dangers during Christmas with tinsel, artificial snow, the tree, etc.

There is more to learn. Keep paper shredders off and unplugged until needed. Check your clothes dryer and washer before closing it. Felines gravitate to warm places. When the weather is cold, stray cats and small animals will even try to find comfort on top of a warm car engine and might not escape in time before it is restarted. Make sure to honk the car horn first.

When you are working with your vet in dealing with a feline problem or medical condition, reliable cat books and different websites can offer a lot of helpful information. Just make sure you share the information with your vet. Also, keep in mind that anyone can have a website.

The vet is the one to ask if you have any questions or in doubt about anything in reference to your pet. This still does not mean you should not do your own research and bring your knowledge, questions, concerns, and common sense to the table.

This is why it is important to find one who will work with you and your pet by answering your questions and satisfying your concerns. This format will also help you to know when you have found the right vet: He should have updated equipment and around-the-clock surveillance of your pet while in his care. You should also check his educational background, certifications, and experience with certain procedures.

Other things to be aware of are never let out a black cat or give it away to just anyone. This also applies to black dogs or any of your black pets because there are people who at any time would do them harm, especially around Halloween.

Never give an animal away free. I would never give an animal away. I am usually the one to whom it is given. There are people who will sell them to research even after posing as a nice family. In addition, they can be used as bait in vicious dogfights. This is why when we would find a lost animal, we were afraid of posting it. When posting, be very careful and do not give too much information. Let them prove they are the owner. We searched the area for posters of lost animals and all websites listing lost and found animals. In addition, we

A BETTER WAY

took the lost pet to our vet to check and scan for any permanent ID. It is important to check the nearest animal shelters in the area and make a report. They might already have a lost report from the owner. Also, you can check the paper ads for lost animals and call the area vets for any of their posted lost pets. Of course, the perfect scenario is to bring a loving owner and their pet together again but be careful and sure, especially if it was posted. Get verification it is their pet such as vet records, photos, pet's license information, etc. Also, get proof of person's ID.

One must also be careful when trying to find a home or shelter for an animal. Things have to be checked. There is a network of people who do care and will help. You can start by getting some names of rescues from your vet's office. It might take a little time, but call these places to investigate. Find out if it is a no-kill shelter or pet rescue. Is a background check done on the adopting person? Do they first visit the new home before validating the adoption and ask to see any vet records to see how well the adopting people take care of their pets? It would be wise to ask around to confirm the information given you by calling another rescue or shelter that is familiar with them. You can also use the internet to find and share information with other animal lovers, rescues, and shelters. You could call a dog rescue of any specific breed of dog, and they will be more than happy to share information about a trustworthy rescue or shelter in the area. If the needy pet is a dog and of the same breed they rescue, they might be able to take him. If they can, then also check on them.

Later, you will feel good you cared enough to overextend yourself in this way. You will see it as a happy ending. There is joy to be found in knowing you are part of the good in this world even if your part is small. I have come to realize some of the most important and significant discoveries I have made in life started out with small and minor endeavors. It is a baby step towards the bigger and better picture. God has made all, big, and small. You do not have to rescue a third world country right away. Start out with one of God's small creatures. If everyone had at the very least this kind of mindset, what a wonderful world it would be!

I see how a small thing can matter not only with animals but also with people in everyday situations. I have found that just a little smile in the right direction can make someone's day better and brighter. While in a checkout line with a full cart, let the person behind you with one or two items go ahead. See how it makes you feel. It is a small gesture but a big thing in itself to think

A BETTER WAY

of others in this kind way. It is the thinking of another outside of one's self, that makes the difference. In reality, you have helped yourself through a wonderful chain reaction of what I like to say is God's karma from his grace and blessings.

    May your sincere care and expressed love, however insignificant, for all of God's creatures ... big and small, help bring you spiritual growth and inner peace.

www.ingramcontent.com/pod-product-compliance
Lightning Source LLC
Chambersburg PA
CBHW040052160426
43192CB00002B/51